W9-CMD-426

DISCARDED BY
MT. LEBANON PUBLIC LIBRARY

Mt. Lebanon Public Library
16 Castle Shannon Blvd.
Pittsburgh, PA 15228-2252
412-531-1912
www.mtlebanonlibrary.org
10/2018

THE
REPUBLICAN
WORKERS
PARTY

Praise for *The Republican Workers Party*

"A big homerun—thanks for all you do!" —Jared Kushner

"An early and confident Trump supporter, Buckley makes a persuasive argument that Trump has reshaped American politics, opening up opportunities for ordinary people which his predecessors blocked off." —Michael Barone

"Buckley is by turns scathing, funny, and sympathetic, but always well informed. The Republican Workers Party whose emergence he describes promotes capitalism without cronies, nationalism without ethnic fascism, and solidarity without immobility. In short, he rolls the stone away from the American heart." —Allen Guelzo

"Dry wit, deep learning, and perspectives that instantly strike you as correct even when they go against everything you've thought before." —Daniel P. McCarthy

"Frank Buckley is one of the most astute observers of the modern American scene." —Deroy Murdock

Praise for *The Republic of Virtue*

"Bracing stuff … his writing is lucid and often witty." —*Wall Street Journal*

"Frank Buckley's new book shows how we can rein in crony capitalism and help restore the Republic." —William J. Bennett

"This is Buckley at his colorful, muckraking best—an intelligent, powerful, but depressing argument laced with humor." —Gordon S. Wood

Praise for *The Way Back*

"Frank Buckley marshals tremendous data and insight in a compelling study." —Francis Fukuyama

"Best book of the year." —Michael Anton

Praise for *The Once and Future King*

"His prose explodes with energy." —James Ceasar

HOW THE **TRUMP VICTORY** DROVE
EVERYONE CRAZY, AND WHY IT WAS
JUST WHAT WE NEEDED

THE
REPUBLICAN
WORKERS
PARTY

F.H. BUCKLEY

Encounter Books
New York • London

Frontispiece: Ford Madox Brown, *Work*, 1852–65

© 2018 by F.H. Buckley

All rights reserved. No part of this publication may be reproduced,
stored in a retrieval system, or transmitted, in any form or by
any means, electronic, mechanical, photocopying, recording,
or otherwise, without the prior written permission of
Encounter Books, 900 Broadway, Suite 601,
New York, New York, 10003.

First American edition published in 2018 by Encounter Books,
an activity of Encounter for Culture and Education, Inc.,
a nonprofit, tax exempt corporation.
Encounter Books website address: www.encounterbooks.com

Manufactured in the United States and printed on
acid-free paper. The paper used in this publication meets
the minimum requirements of ANSI/NISO Z39.48–1992
(R 1997) (*Permanence of Paper*).

FIRST AMERICAN EDITION

LIBRARY OF CONGRESS CATALOGING-IN-PUBLICATION DATA
Names: Buckley, F. H. (Francis H.), 1948– author.
Title: The Republican Workers Party : how the Trump victory drove
everyone crazy, and why it was just what we needed / by F.H. Buckley.
Description: New York : Encounter Books, [2018] |
Includes bibliographical references and index.
Identifiers: LCCN 2018003456 (print) | LCCN 2018028066 (ebook) |
ISBN 9781641770071 (ebook) | ISBN 9781641770064 (hardcover : alk. paper)
Subjects: LCSH: United States—Politics and government—2017– |
Republican Party (U.S. : 1854–) | Trump, Donald, 1946–
Classification: LCC E913 (ebook) | LCC E913 .B83 2018 (print) |
DDC 324.2734—dc23
LC record available at https://lccn.loc.gov/2018003456

Interior page design and composition: BooksByBruce.com

For Esther, Sarah, Nick and Benjamin Herbert

CONTENTS

CHAPTER 1

HOW THE HELL DID WE GET HERE?

Everything begins in mystique, and ends in politics.
—Charles Péguy, *Notre jeunesse*

Americans are the most generous and admirable of people, and among the worst governed in the First World. Can our problems be fixed? I don't know. How did they come about? That is a question I think I can answer.

I arrived in America in 1989, an immigrant from Canada. My America was the country of John Ford's westerns, a country of people hard on the outside and soft on the inside. Though they lived in a heartless world, Americans were secret romantics, like Humphrey Bogart in *Casablanca*, who never abandoned their illusions. Theirs was a country touched by grace, as Dallas and the Ringo Kid were in *Stagecoach*, one that always gave people a second chance. It was a country of loud exuberance and quiet nobility.

It was a country whose troops provided the margin of victory in two world wars, whose commitment to ideals of freedom and justice inspired everyone, everywhere. It was a country of unrivaled prosperity, with the greatest educational system in the world. It had owned the twentieth century and was the desired destination country for every emigrant. It was the country that, as Churchill once said, always did the right thing in the end, though only after it had tried everything else.

But in recent times America has no longer seemed able to do the right thing in the end. On cross-country rankings of economic freedom, we had been dropping like a stone. Annual growth rates had fallen to 1 or 2 percent, which the IMF managing director, Christine Lagarde, called the "new mediocre."[1] Our K–12 schools were dismal failures compared with those of other First World countries. Our bureaucrats had made themselves into a parallel government, an unelected and unaccountable administrative state. We had saddled ourselves with wasteful laws, which seemed impossible to repeal in Washington's gridlock. We had become more divided, each group sequestered in its hates.

Conservatives knew that change must come. After the excesses of the first Obama Congress, the Tea Party election of 2010 gave Republicans control of the House of Representatives. Fine, they were told, but you're still stuck with the Affordable Care Act (Obamacare) until you win the White House and the Senate. After an embarrassing loss in the presidential election of 2012, Republicans won the Senate in 2014. Close, but no cigar; you still need the White House. Then came the 2016 presidential election.

Both Republicans and Democrats thought that the election of Donald Trump would change everything. Trump's supporters hoped it would mean a sharp break from twenty years of foreign policy failures, an end to both George W. Bush's nation building and Obama's feckless-ness. We wouldn't go looking for foreign countries to invade, and we wouldn't be erasing any of our red lines. We'd be neither a naïf nor a patsy.

Republican voters knew that our K–12 schools and immigration laws were badly in need of reform, and they liked Trump's plans for them. They wanted Trump to cut the administrative state and all its wasteful, job-destroying regulations down to size. Mostly, they knew that we had become a class society where rich parents raised rich kids and poor parents raised poor kids, and that this was a betrayal of the American Dream, the idea that whoever you are and wherever you come from, your children will have it better than you did. They knew that this promise had been broken, and that Trump had pledged to renew it. That is why they elected him president.

Democrats also knew that Trump had promised change, but change was not what they wanted. The administrative state that employed so many of them, directly and indirectly, suited them just fine. So did all the barriers to mobility in our ossified class society. If immobility meant that middle-class kids wouldn't get ahead, it also meant that their own kids wouldn't fall behind. They'd go to the best schools and in time would take their places in an American *noblesse*. That is how an American aristocracy was created out of the well-credentialed, liberal elite atop the greasy pole, a privileged group that Christopher Lasch, and before him Milovan Djilas, called the New Class.[2]

They are mostly liberals, but they also include people like George W. Bush (son of George H. W.), John Podhoretz (son of Norman) and Bill Kristol (son of Irving). When Jeb Bush looked like the Republican heir apparent, and Hillary Clinton the Democratic candidate, the class divide between the elite and ordinary Americans recalled the French aristocracies of old.

The New Class isn't composed of the super-wealthy, the top 0.1 percent of earners, who are surprisingly egalitarian and have typically pulled themselves up by their bootstraps. It isn't the basketball million-aires or the high-tech gazillionaires we're talking about. Rather, it's the rest of the top 10 percent, the professionals earning more than $200,000 a year, whose toast always falls butter side up and who pass on their advantages to their children. They are adept in the hypertechnical rules and ever-changing Newspeak employed to exclude the backward, the eccentric, the politically incorrect. Their beliefs are liberal, their speech is socially approved and they never tell jokes. They live in a world divided between people *at* the table and people *on* the table, between sources and targets. You will know them by their mating calls. Reproductive freedom. The world is flat. All are welcome here.

People who seek to explain Trump often look for parallels from our past. He's a new Andrew Jackson, they tell us, or perhaps a plain-speaking Harry Truman. Some on the right compare him to Ronald Reagan, since everyone on the right loves Ronald Reagan. But he's unlike anything we've seen before, for the simple reason that he's up against something we've never seen before: a liberalism that has given up on the American Dream of a mobile and classless society. And that brought us to the paradox of the 2016 election, when the liberal candidate of a counterrevolutionary and aristocratic New Class was defeated by a revolutionary capitalist offering a path to social mobility.

Like all aristocrats, the New Class defends its privileges as the consequence of fixed and unchangeable laws of nature. If you've fallen behind, it's because of the shift to an information economy with its premium wages for high-skilled workers, and regrettably you're dumb and low-skilled. If you've fared poorly, maybe you did it to yourself, with your drug dependency, your laziness, your general loutishness.

We'd love to do something for you poor slobs, they say, but nothing can be done.

Except that we didn't get an aristocracy from the laws of nature. Rather, we got it because of artificial and unjust rules and institutions, including the broken schools and regulatory barriers that liberals support. When they say it can't be changed, that's nothing more than a self-serving mythology, of the sort that Herbert Marcuse, Max Horkheimer, Theodor Adorno and the Frankfurt School were targeting in their left-wing critique of capitalism. They too had been told that power relationships were cast in stone and that nothing could be done about it: "Justified in the guise of brutal facts as something eternally immutable to intervention, the social injustice from which those facts arise is as sacrosanct today as the medicine man once was under the protection of his gods."³

The Frankfurt School wasn't buying it. A false narrative had legitimized an unjustly privileged class, they said, and it could be undone. They told us that transformative change was possible, but they never did show us how we'd get to the promised land. Their socialist ideals were impenetrably dense and devoid of the most basic understanding of economics. It turned out to be a dead end. What the Frankfurt School did understand, however, was the need to reject what must never be accepted: false narratives, injustice, aristocracy.

That was good advice. But now things are reversed. Yesterday's revolutionaries have come to power and become today's counterrevolutionaries. They are Bourbons who seek to pass themselves off as Jacobins. They have bought into a radical leftism, while resisting the call to unseat a patrician class that leftists in the past would have opposed. They tell us that aristocracy is natural, and that they deserve their place at the top of the totem pole.

Trump said it could be changed, that we could return to an America where our children—not just the children of privilege—will have it better than we did. We could do this by fixing our schools, reforming our immigration laws and draining a regulatory swamp. He said that his opponent was corrupt and had given up on the promise of America. That is how to understand the Trump revolution. That is why he won.

And now? Things never turn out exactly as we hoped or feared, as Charles Péguy observed. Trump's supporters wake up each morning wondering what fresh hell was tweeted at 3:00 a.m. The pace of new appointments is slow, and Trump loyalists have seen administration jobs go to the careerists whom Jeb Bush (and perhaps even Hillary Clinton) might have hired. Some of the appointments, like that of Anthony Scaramucci, would have been thought laughable in a comic-opera Ruritania. At the White House, we've been treated to a succession of feckless amateurs, flaming egomaniacs and shady hustlers. The tax reform of 2017 will bring back jobs, but the wretched carried interest perk for hedge fund managers remains. Trump had campaigned against it, but was no match for the K Street lobbyists and a complicit Republican establishment that supported it. There's always a discrepancy between the vision and the reality.

Since the election change has been coming, however, even if a media clamoring for impeachment has ignored it. We've added three million new jobs; and the stock market, which Paul Krugman said would "never" recover after the election, increased by a third in the space of a year. Consumer confidence is at its highest level since 2000. Trump has made good on his promise to replace Justice Scalia with a Supreme Court replacement in his mold, and is filling up federal court vacancies with judicial conservatives. He has withdrawn from the Paris Climate Accord and greenlighted the Keystone Pipeline. We've stopped adding wasteful new regulations and have begun the slow process of undoing the costly ones that have weakened our economy. As attorney general, Jeff Sessions has reversed the anti-police biases of the Obama administration and embraced tough-on-crime policies. Illegal immigration has dropped by 60 percent and is at the lowest level in this century.

Yet every time things have seemed to turn his way, Trump has made an equal and opposite gaffe. Firmness and prudence, energy and tact, were not given to him in equal measure; and the man who wrote *The Art of the Deal* now finds himself obliged to deal with people who can scarcely hide their contempt for him. Amidst charges of anti-Trump bias, the probe by the special counsel, Robert Mueller, grinds on like the mills of the gods, but thus far without producing anything more than pleas to technical offenses. We've also had to deal with the creeps and the crazies, the white nationalists who seek to pass themselves off as authentic Trump supporters. The defeat of Roy Moore in the 2017 election for U.S. senator from Alabama, a state where Trump won 63 percent of the vote, has shown that the change desired by Trump supporters was change within the bounds of normal human behavior. That shouldn't have been a surprise.

The bumps in the road have encouraged some to hope that things might revert to the status quo ante, with two complacent political parties ignoring the issues that got Trump elected. But thoughtful people in both parties know that indifference and complacency won't work. That is something Theresa May in Britain discovered when she nearly lost to the impossible Jeremy Corbin.

Whatever might happen to Trump, the causes he identified will continue to dominate American politics. That is the subject of this book: how he triumphed over a tone-deaf Republican establishment and created a new party that he called the Republican Workers Party. And it is about how I witnessed the death of the old Republican Party and assisted at the new party's birth.

I

A NEW PARTY IS BORN

It will therefore be necessary for me in this book to disclose, not only those things which have hitherto remained undivulged, but also the causes of those occurrences which have already been described.

— Procopius, *The Secret History*

CHAPTER 2

A TIME FOR CHOOSING

In June 2015, when Donald Trump came down the escalator at the Trump Tower to announce his candidacy, nearly everyone thought it was a joke. We felt that our presidents should have a background in politics or the military. He had neither. Instead, he had the celebrity that came from a reality TV show, and before then the celebrity of being a celebrity. He didn't speak with a plummy accent. He said things that shocked people. He mocked a war hero, John McCain; he called an American judge a "Mexican"; he gave his opponents insulting nicknames. And he was just what the Republicans needed.

From the start I was intrigued by Trump. I liked his business smarts, his flamboyance, the contrast with all the gray suits in the Republican Party. His rudeness took getting used to, but there is such a thing as repressive politeness when it prevents a discussion of legitimate problems. And Trump was talking about issues that affected the everyday lives of voters—job losses, bad schools, immigration—and that were impolite to mention. Trump also communicated vitality and authenticity, in contrast to Hillary Clinton's stumbles, her formaldehyde-frozen face, her inhuman cackles of laughter. Crucially, only Trump could defeat Clinton, I thought. For that insight I'll give myself full marks, since it eluded nearly everyone else until 11:00 p.m. on November 8, 2016.

I heard Republicans tell me of this or that sin Trump had committed, and I wanted to ask them how things had turned out when they nominated a Latter-Day Saint. I listened to everything that Democrats said about Trump's all-too-human failings, and I wanted to say, "These are all excellent arguments, but have you perhaps forgotten how despicable your candidate is?" Because defeating Hillary Clinton was what it was all about.

HOW WE REACHED A DEAD END

With Hillary Clinton, the Democrats chose the most corrupt American politician since Aaron Burr. Peter Schweizer's *Clinton Cash* revealed how the Clinton Foundation had seemingly sold off American foreign policy to the highest bidder.[1] Even the *New York Times* concluded that "it was hard to tell where the foundation ended and the State Department began."[2] According to a nonpartisan watchdog group, the foundation seemed like a slush fund for the Clintons themselves.[3] It all looked like pay-for-play, and when Hillary had nothing left to trade away, the contributions began to dry up.

If she were to be elected president, I thought, we would likely see America descend to Third World levels of public corruption. I recalled how Lois Lerner's Exempt Organizations unit at the IRS had denied charitable status to conservative groups, how Obama had told us there was "not even a smidgen of corruption" behind the affair,[4] and how the *New York Times* had walked back its initial criticism of the IRS on the matter.[5] I also recalled how the IRS inspector general was attacked for disclosing the scandal.[6] I thought that Hillary Clinton was vastly more mean-spirited and less principled than Obama, and more vindictive than Richard Nixon; that as president she would happily use all the tools at her disposal to silence dissent, and that the progressive media would cheer her on as she did so.

Like the insufferable Tracy Flick in the dark comedy *Election*, Clinton thought she deserved to win and couldn't understand why she wasn't fifty points ahead. We owed it to her, and the slogan "I'm with Her" signaled that the onus was on us to prove our virtue by voting for her. When we failed to do so, her bitterness and utter lack of introspection were chillingly on display in a postelection book that blamed the voters for being unworthy of her.[7]

The late Michael Kelly called her "Saint Hillary," a woman who wanted to lead nothing less than a moral reformation. "A lot of people, contemplating such a task, might fall prey to self-doubts," said Kelly. "Mrs. Clinton does not blink."[8] Reportedly, she now wants to become a Methodist minister. Given her inflated self-regard and her desire to preach to fallen humanity, that's not surprising, but a cynical Baudelaire might wonder why she is permitted to enter a church. What conversation could she have with God?[9]

If she had won, we would have come to resemble a Third World country not just in our corruption, but in continuing the slide toward one-man presidential rule that began with Obama. "I've got a pen and a phone," he had proclaimed, as he proceeded to bypass Congress through executive orders that substituted for legislation. When the Republicans took control of the House of Representatives in 2011, Obama discovered that gridlock was his friend, as it let him rule by diktat whenever he picked a quarrel with Speaker John Boehner. Obama has a special talent in picking quarrels, and Mrs. Clinton would have found it easier still to quarrel with people for whom she openly displayed her contempt.

I wrote a book about the temptation to monarchism in presidential regimes and called it *The Once and Future King*.[10] That's where I thought America was heading, unless we could somehow recover our republican principles. But how could that be done?

THE REPUBLICAN WORKERS PARTY EMERGES

November 2016 was a time for choosing. We had to take sides. "You must wager," wrote Blaise Pascal. "It is not optional. You are embarked."[11] Not to choose was to opt for continuing the descent to an unacceptable future. Nor were false choices permitted, the perfect Republican candidate who could never get elected, the return to sunny uplands in 2020. Those were simply cop-outs. And even if our favored candidate won in the end, there would still be messy compromises and no better than partial victories, since every administration is staffed by careerists who have mortgages but not principles.

Nevertheless, we had a choice in 2016, between the status quo and disruption. For Democrats, the status quo was Hillary Clinton; for Republicans, it was the designated losers who would play the role of the Washington Generals to her Harlem Globetrotters. Disruption meant Donald Trump or Bernie Sanders. As it turned out, Sanders wasn't really an option, since the Democratic establishment conspired to ensure that he wouldn't get the nomination. Even before she won the Democratic nomination, Clinton controlled the party's purse strings and could count on superdelegates at the convention to put her over the top. That's how she beat a seventy-five-year-old socialist who as a senator hadn't even called himself a Democrat. Had the Republicans played those tricks, their nominee would have been Jeb Bush.

There was a curious overlap between Trump and Sanders. Both were concerned about bad trade deals and crony capitalism, and they even shared a concern about immigration. Both saw an America divided unjustly along class lines, and they promised to change the policies that harmed the bottom 90 percent of Americans. Both spoke to pressing economic issues, unlike Hillary Clinton with her identity politics. Both aspired to lead a party of American workers. Had some of Sanders's disappointed voters not stayed home on Election Day, Trump might well have lost.

On many issues, Trump and Sanders had a common view of what ailed America. They both understood the ways in which ordinary Americans had been left behind by the elites in both parties. They both had the same goal of an economically mobile and just society. The difference was that Sanders would have employed socialist means to achieve socialist goals, while Trump proposed capitalist means to do so.

Trump had the better argument, I knew. We're not going to make workers better off through 90 percent marginal taxes, worker-owned cooperatives and green energy boondoggles. We're not going to produce jobs for employees by beating up on employers. We're not even going to fix things by spending more on welfare. It's easy to forget just how generous our safety net is. Perhaps we don't spend it wisely, but spend it we do, in 126 federal antipoverty programs, not to mention a host of state and city programs, totaling nearly a trillion dollars in 2012 according to the Cato Institute's Michael Tanner.[12] The Heritage Foundation reported that the average household headed by someone who lacks a high school degree received more than $46,000 in benefits and services while paying $11,500 in taxes.[13] As a percentage of GDP, the United States spends more than all but four European countries, and just a little less than Sweden.[14]

I liked Sanders's emphasis on inequality and immobility, but saw that he didn't know how to fix it. And then it all came together for me at a dinner with a Republican congressman in 2015. He was complaining about the members of the House's rambunctious and very conservative

Freedom Caucus. "Right-wing Marxists," he called them. Aha, I thought. That's me.

I am a Marxist to the extent that I see America divided into different classes and think this as a revolutionary time. An aristocratic counter-revolutionary class is arrayed against a set of voters with a revolutionary consciousness who believe in the possibility of transformative change. It is like 1917, except that now it's the Left that is counterrevolutionary, wanting to keep things as they are, unjust, unequal.

And that's why mine is a right-wing Marxism. It wasn't free-market capitalism that made us immobile. Instead, it was all the barriers to advancement that liberals created, through statutes and regulations that place a stumbling block in the path of those who seek to rise. Today it's the socialist who is objectively counterrevolutionary, for there's nothing more truly revolutionary than a capitalist system that opens its doors to industry and talent, that erases unearned privileges.

There's another sense in which I'm a Marxist. I see public policy questions through an economic prism. I don't deny that culture matters, that children need two-parent families, that drug dependency holds people back; I simply don't think that the state can do much to change those things, except to make them worse. David Hume wasn't far off the mark when he observed that "all plans of government, which suppose great reformation in the manners of mankind, are plainly imaginary."[15] Today the only moral rearmament crusade we need from the government is one that gives people real jobs. After that, we can take care of ourselves.

A job is more than a means of survival, more than the contribution of labor to the economy. It's also the difference between earned self-respect and the shame of unemployment and dependency. It's the companionship of fellow workers versus the solitude of the unemployed. It's the difference between the purposeful and the purposeless life. In our lives we play several different roles, but not the least is man the creator, man the producer. *Homo faber.*

Jobs is what Trump pledged. When he announced his candidacy he said, "I will be the greatest jobs president that God ever created." When he complained about our trade deals, he said that our labor participation rate is so low "because China has our jobs and Mexico has our jobs." When he spoke of immigration, he told us that illegal immigrants were taking jobs away from Americans. When he promised to rebuild our infrastructure, he was talking about jobs for workers. When he mentioned his Republican opponents, he noted that "they don't talk jobs."

> I watch the speeches of these people, and they say the sun will rise, the moon will set, all sorts of wonderful things will happen. And people are saying, "What's going on? I just want a job. Just get me a job. I don't need the rhetoric. I want a job."

Hillary Clinton despised ordinary Americans, but we supported the candidate who reached out to workers in jobless inner cities, to union members at the plant and to the unemployed coal miners.

It was messy, to be sure. Trump at times reminds one of how Henry Adams had described an unreflective Teddy Roosevelt as pure act, "the quality that mediæval theology ascribed to God."[16] And when the alternative was a continuing slide to mediocrity and an unjust class society, action seemed better than inaction. But Trump was much more than pure act. From his campaign and from the family members and advisors I would meet, there would come an entirely new political party, one with a preferential option for the lower 90 percent of Americans, for people who needed secure jobs with good wages.

We were creating what Trump called a "workers party" when a reporter asked him what the Republican Party would become under him. "You're going to have a worker's party. A party of people that haven't had a real wage increase in 18 years, that are angry."[17] At the 2017 CPAC conference he called it the Republican Workers Party. It would be something never before seen in America, something that would get him elected president, something that the pundits entirely missed.

The Republican Workers Party would be libertarian in its opposition to crony capitalism but economically liberal when it comes to welfare policies for those truly in need. It would be a party of nationalists who reject a globalism that is indifferent between the welfare of Americans and of foreigners. It would be a jobs party led by a jobs president. More than anything else, it would be a party that seeks to restore the American Dream of a country where our children will have it better than we did.

During the campaign I became a part of the story. I worked on the Trump campaign, I wrote speeches for him and his family, I advised on transition matters, and I came to understand the revolution in American politics. It fit like a glove, because I had provided the same account of what needed to be done in my 2016 book, *The Way Back: Restoring the Promise of America*.[18] The previous year I had told Trump that my forthcoming book would pin American decline on a New Class of liberal aristocrats who want to keep us economically immobile. The Left had created the problem, but conservatives had failed to blame them for creating the kind of class society that's wholly at odds with the idea of America. We need to take the gloves off, I said. Evidently Trump didn't need any persuading.

CHAPTER 3

THE CAMPAIGN TAKES SHAPE

The other Republican candidates played by the rules. Not Trump. At their first debate in August 2015, he was the only one who refused to pledge that he would support the nominee, whomever he was. That's it, said Frank Luntz, a Republican pollster. He just destroyed his candidacy. You have to be a nice guy to win the nomination. But the only person who was hurt was Luntz himself, for Trump tweeted back, "don't come to my office looking for business again." As for the other candidates on the stage, Jeb Bush, Ted Cruz and John Kasich all declined to support the Republican candidate in the November election. They were the pledge breakers, not Trump.

Moments later in the debate, Megyn Kelly called Trump out for labeling women he didn't like as "fat pigs, dogs, slobs, and disgusting animals," and suggested he was "part of the war on women." That would have produced a groveling apology from any of the other sixteen candidates on stage, but then Trump wasn't like any of them. Here's what he said:

> I don't frankly have time for total political correctness. And to be honest with you, this country doesn't have time either. This country is in big trouble. We don't win anymore. We lose to China. We lose to Mexico both in trade and at the border. We lose to everybody.

Someone, somewhere coined the term "virtue signaling." That's where you let everyone know just how moral, how refined, how well tamed you are. But that wasn't Trump's style. Instead he went out of his way to show his contempt for political correctness. He signaled that he couldn't care less about conventional political pieties, and that's what voters were waiting for. They wanted a change artist and knew they wouldn't get that from someone who was cowed by Megyn Kelly. They wanted a person who was going to break things they thought needed breaking, and Trump was the only one who showed he could do it. If others wanted to signal how virtuous they were, he was going to signal his toughness.

That was the rude and exciting campaign to which I signed on. Sometimes I felt a wee bit like Hyman Roth in *The Godfather Part II*. "I said to myself, this is the business we have chosen." But I really wasn't overly bothered by Trump's breaches of decorum. Like other Trump supporters, I thought that Republicans had been too polite, and I wanted to see a few rules broken. When Simone de Beauvoir wrote her autobiography, she called it the *Mémoires d'une jeune fille rangée*, which means the memoirs of a proper, well-behaved little girl. That's how Trump supporters saw Jeb Bush, whom the Republican establishment and its donors had anointed as the nominee, and who proved how little they all mattered in the end. Bush won only three of the 2,472 convention delegates, each one costing him $50 million in campaign spending. At the convention they wandered around, a little confused, looking for people to talk to.

WHAT I SAW OF THE REVOLUTION

I took a circuitous route getting to The Donald. There were not, I think, many other campaign workers born in Saskatchewan, the Canadian prairie province at the back of the North Wind that's easy to draw and hard to pronounce. But then many of us come from odd places, and sometimes that gives us an edge. It did so for the Duke of Wellington. When someone slighted his Irish birthplace, he replied that "not everyone born in a manger is a mule."

I had grown up in a classless society but was still a child of privilege. We were nearly all children of privilege, the Canadian and American boomer kids of my generation, compared with our Depression-era parents and those who came after us. We got a decent high school education, and if we went on to college we found tuition affordable. In either case, there were good jobs waiting for us. Marriage, children and house purchases followed, in an ordered and accustomed manner.

I taught law at McGill and only left Montreal in 1989 when I received a better offer from an American school. The same sort of thing had happened to many Canadians before me, as John Kenneth Galbraith noted, when our devotion to the British monarchy was trumped by a five-dollar-a-day pay differential. Thereafter, we're embarrassingly slow to naturalize. Why bother, we think, when the two countries are so similar? The Russians, the Venezuelans, they hop to it, but I dawdled, and it wasn't until 2014 that I became a U.S. citizen.

I had always paid close attention to U.S. politics, even in Canada. But you look at things differently after you become a citizen. First, of course, you'll want to roll up the immigration wall to keep out the damn foreigners. And then you might want to exercise your constitutional right to petition the government for redress of grievances. That's how I came to work on the Trump campaign.

While teaching at the George Mason law school, I was also a senior editor at the *American Spectator*. That didn't give me a seat at the cool kids' table in the conservative lunchroom, but for more than ten years I had directed an educational program for federal judges and I came to be good friends with many of them. When I heard that Trump had plans to release a list of possible candidates for the Supreme Court, I therefore passed on a few names to him and to Senator Jeff Sessions.

With the list of judges, I appended a draft speech, prepared by my wife Esther Goldberg, the *American Spectator*'s Bob Tyrrell and me. Esther had written an op-ed defending Trump for the *Spectator* that Rush Limbaugh had read over the air, and Bob is a longtime hero of the conservative movement whose magazine was the only pro-Trump journal in town. Soon after, Jared Kushner and Stephen Miller put our little writing team to work on other speeches. Jared was married to Ivanka Trump, Donald Trump's daughter; and Stephen Miller had come from the office of Senator Sessions to work on the Trump campaign. We spoke often with Kushner and Miller on the phone and shared hundreds of emails.

We were unpaid volunteers, but we still had a ringside seat on the campaign. We had prepared a draft of the foreign policy speech that Trump delivered at Washington's Mayflower Hotel in April 2016, where

we suggested a reset with Russia,[1] and a sharp break from prior thinking on external affairs. We sat in the second row of the hotel ballroom,
pinching ourselves when we heard Trump say, "If President Obama's
goal had been to weaken America, he could not have done a better job."
Or, "we're in a war against radical Islam, but President Obama won't
even name the enemy!" And best of all, "And then there's ISIS. I have
a simple message for them. Their days are numbered. I won't tell them
where and I won't tell them how." When the speech was over we repaired
to a reception, where I sat at a table with a group of preening big shots.
"I can tell you who wrote that speech," they assured me. They mentioned
names I had never heard of. Nobody had a clue about us.

I wasn't under any great illusions about our role. We had provided
ideas that would have been expressed without us, lines that someone
else would have written. But we also learned how the campaign insiders thought. We knew what they'd want to do were Trump elected, and
best of all I saw that we had the same understanding as Trump about
American decline and the failures of conservatism. We knew that Trump
alone could rescue what was living from what was dead in American
conservatism, and we knew how he would do it.

Trump realized what other conservatives had ignored: that the
American Dream of a mobile and classless society was broken. He told
us that an economic elite had unjustly risen atop what was supposed to
be an egalitarian and mobile society. He understood that corruption was
a silent killer of the economy, that it has given America a wasteful regime
of crony capitalism that transfers wealth from outsiders to insiders; and
unlike other Republicans he proposed to do something about it. He also
complained of twenty years of foreign policy blunders that allowed our
enemies to mock us and encouraged our friends to mistrust us, and said
he wanted to make America great again.

Those ideas informed the speeches we wrote for Trump. All were well
received, especially the convention speech I prepared for Donald Trump,
Jr., which laid the blame for income immobility on the Democrats.

> The other party also tells us they believe in the American Dream. They
> say we should worry about economic inequality and immobility. You
> know what? They're right. But what they don't tell you is that it was
> their policies that caused the problem.

It went over well, but within an hour someone discovered that a line in the speech had appeared in something I had written for the *American Conservative* magazine. I had repeated myself without realizing it. (People of a certain age are apt to do this.) The day before, Melania Trump had given a speech that resembled one Michelle Obama had given, and now the Trump family seemed to have done it again. So I quickly revealed that I had written both the article and the speech, and that therefore no one had plagiarized anyone. For the next three hours, I took phone calls from around the world, until the press realized that, sadly, there was no scandal. I had my 180 minutes of fame, but the only person who enjoyed this was Dan McCarthy, the amiable editor of the *American Conservative*, who gleefully tweeted a link to the article.[2]

A SOLDIER IN THE REPUBLICAN CIVIL WAR

My unmasking as a Trump supporter didn't win me any friends in my little circle of conservatives, almost all of whom hated Trump. They were libertarians who wanted wide-open borders to admit anyone who wanted to come here. They were free traders who worried that tariffs harmed American consumers but weren't much interested in American producers or workers. They obsessed over the small stuff, things like eminent domain and British libel laws, while ignoring the much greater issues that had caused our decline on measures of economic freedom put out by right-wing think tanks such as the Cato Institute.

Establishment conservatives saw the Trump insurgency as a second storming of the Winter Palace. They called themselves "NeverTrumpers," and tried everything they could think of to defeat him. They rallied around one Republican opponent and then another, and when that failed they tried to persuade his convention delegates to switch sides, and when that failed they looked for a third-party candidate to oppose him, and when that failed they encouraged presidential electors to break their pledges. It was one long, hysterical temper tantrum. Prisoners of a callous ideology, they objected to Trump's concern for the welfare of ordinary Americans, and ignored his essential conservatism. If today they criticize Democrats, I'm minded to warn them that they might be providing aid and comfort to the hated Donald Trump. Mostly, however, they've remained fixated on Trump's failings, for which liberals accord them the respect normally reserved for conservatives only after their death.

Trump has an extraordinary ability to bring out the worst in his opponents, to turn them into Gadarene swine. When he goes low, they always go lower, and with all the hardness of the self-righteous the NeverTrumpers employed every vile epithet to describe him and his followers. Witless ape, dog crap, cancer, caudillo, ignoramus, moron, those were some of the nicer things they called him. Rich Lowry, the editor of *National Review*, is normally the gentlest of people, but he enthused that, in a debate with Trump, Carly Fiorina had "cut his balls off." In their hatred of Trump and their descent into vulgarity, Trump's right-wing critics had lost their minds and their manners; and I began to love Trump for his enemies.

The NeverTrumpers hated Trump's message, his accent, his hair. They hated the Trump Tower and Mar-a-Lago. They hated his supporters. Mostly they hated being ignored. In "The Second Coming," William Butler Yeats described how they felt.

> Turning and turning in the widening gyre
> The falcon cannot hear the falconer
> Things fall apart.

The elite writers had imagined themselves conservatism's falconers, its controllers, its chief ideologues and commissars of ideological purity; but Trump was the falcon that had slipped their commands. In their think tanks, their little magazines, the conservative establishment thought it had ownership rights to the Republican Party, at least to its thinking component, and it was a psychic blow to be cold-shouldered. The falcon did not hear them, and mere anarchy was loosed on the world.

The NeverTrumpers were right about one thing, however. Trump was not a doctrinaire right-winger. When he was accused of being something other than a conservative, Trump said, "it's called the Republican Party, not the Conservative Party." Conservative ideologues had proposed that Social Security be privatized, but Trump wanted none of that. We have a generous welfare policy, and all that Trump planned to do was make it work better. Most Americans were with him on that, and not with the NeverTrumpers. I debated Rich Lowry, and quoted to him Anton Chigurh's line in *No Country for Old Men*. "If the rule you followed brought you to this, of what use was the rule?"

The NeverTrumpers belonged to a party of beautiful losers, one that should have won the presidency in 2012. But time had passed them by. They lived in the glow of past triumphs, and made a cargo cult of their 1980 briefing books. Keepers of the flame, they preached a perfect fidelity to right-wing principles, but what the voters sensed was an indifference to people. All their fine ideas had gotten them nowhere.

There were ten candidates for the presidency in 2012, serious people such as Mitt Romney, Newt Gingrich and Rick Perry. All shared their party's anxiety about protecting the ultra-rich and opposed anything that looked like a tax hike. Early on, at one of their campaign debates, they were asked whether they'd agree to a grand tax reform bargain that would give them everything they wanted, eliminating every wretched interest group perk, every inefficient subsidy, so long as they agreed to raise taxes on those earning more than $250,000 a year—and every one of them said no. Perhaps, like Romney, they thought that $250,000 was a middle-class income.[3]

When the party nominated Romney, it thought it had sealed the deal. He was the perfect Republican from central casting, with Tom Dewey's good looks, the Koch brothers' money and Karl Rove's strategic smarts. What could go wrong? And then in the middle of the campaign Romney issued a 160-page booklet with 59—count 'em, 59—separate policy proposals to spur economic growth. The little book was smack-jab full of sensible ideas, from the smartest people at the D.C. think tanks, but nobody paid any attention to it. Here's what they heard instead, a talk Romney gave to some right-wing donors about the 53 percent of high-value "makers" versus the 47 percent of low-value "takers."

> There are 47 percent of the people who will vote for [Obama] no matter what. All right, there are 47 percent who are with him, who are dependent upon government, who believe that they are victims, who believe that government has a responsibility to care for them, who believe that they are entitled to health care, to food, to housing, to you name it.

Romney was simply parroting what people at right-wing think tanks say to each other when they think no one is listening. But when the talk became public, it was the defining moment of the campaign,[4] the death rattle of the old Republican Party. If Romney thought that nearly half of the voters were "takers" from the schnorrer's table who would never support him, he had seemingly just conceded the election. Against stupidity, the gods themselves contend in vain, said Friedrich Schiller. And he hadn't even met a Republican!

Romney had also revealed a contempt for ordinary Americans, since the "takers" included the infirm, the elderly, those who had paid their way in the past and those who could not find work despite their best efforts; but all were seen as shiftless wastrels. Moreover, the 47 percent figure didn't even include those who had benefited from the disguised government subsidies of what Suzanne Mettler calls the "submerged state," especially the home mortgage interest deduction and the capital gains treatment for executive bonus plans that disproportionately benefit the wealthy.[5]

And so the 59-point plan was ignored, and voters instead listened to Obama. In a troubled economy, he told voters that he had their back, while Romney came across as the boss about to hand you the pink slip. The Republicans weren't interested in inequality—but inequality was interested in them. And Obama won.

In a firing squad, it's only the prisoner who doesn't hear the click of the rifles. After the election, a still-baffled Republican establishment commissioned a self-study to learn from their mistakes. Written by party insiders, the report reads like a satire about a clueless political class, the sort of thing the Soviets used to put out about how, for the tenth consecutive time, bad weather had spoiled their five-year plan. The message it conveyed was that Republicans should embrace diversity the next time around, and compete with Democrats in their outreach to minority identity groups.

With Marco Rubio in mind, the study cheerfully noted, "It is encouraging that there are many Republican leaders both in the House and the Senate working on immigration proposals," code language for amnesty. "We must embrace and champion comprehensive immigration reform." It's what the U.S. Chamber of Commerce and other business groups wanted: cheap labor. To hell with American workers. But when the party nominated the man who said "Build the Wall," all their efforts were tossed out the window. In particular, the self-study was laughably out of touch when it said the key to electoral success was "developing and tailoring a message that is non-inflammatory and inclusive to all."

The least inflammatory group around was the "Reformocons," a group of *bien rangé* young conservatives brimming with advice on how Republicans might recover from their 2012 defeat, led by people such as Marco Rubio. In the 1950s, a British satirist named Stephen Potter anticipated them in a series of amusing little books—*Gamesmanship, Supermanship*—on how to get through life with the maximum of success and the minimum of accomplishments. In one of them, Potter took on the "Angry Young Men" of the day, people such as John Braine, John Osborne and Kingsley Amis, writers who had mocked a complacent British establishment; and in response Potter came up with a group of "mild young men." They were people like his vicar, who would hold his teacup with two fingers and say things like, "But I see value in that too!" The Reformocons were also mild young men, intelligent, sensible and bloodless. If they're forgotten today, it's because they hadn't understood the popular outrage at how we've become a class society; and had failed to recognize that, as the barriers to mobility were all erected by the Left, it should have been their issue to seize.

Things move on. To everything there is a season. That fine old family firm, the pride of Fifth Avenue, started out as a one-room country store. Dig back into its history and you'll find a crusty old founder with dirt under his fingernails who saw his chances and took 'em. If the better sort of people sniffed at his methods, he succeeded where they had failed, and unlike them he had a heart as big as a whale. His children, with their fancy-pants MBAs, inherited a going concern and were lucky enough to be there for the payoff. But now new challengers, new upstarts, threaten the core business—and of the grandchildren on Ritalin it is best not to speak.

It's entropy, the second law of thermodynamics, a system's gradual and inevitable dissipation of energy. The same thing happens in the world of ideas. Pick any great intellectual movement, one that seems so well established, and you'll find the same cycle of innovation, stasis and decrepitude. The right-wing think tanks had told us that they were the brains of conservatism, its idea factories. But in many cases the brains had stopped working and they had become the movement's stomach.

They gorged on the money they raised from conservative donors, as Jeb Bush had, with about the same political impact.

The NeverTrumpers never saw it coming. Before the election some of them assembled a blacklist of Trump "collaborators" to be purged after his defeat. More in sorrow than in anger, Matt Walsh gave NeverTrumpers their marching orders, in Glenn Beck's *The Blaze*. "As unpleasant a task as it may be, I think we need to identify the traitors and remember their names. We do this not out of spite, but in keeping with the Bible's many warnings about false prophets." Trump support-ers might be pardoned if we begged for forgiveness, but our betrayal of conservatism would never be forgotten.

Sadly, I was never so prominent as to merit a place on the blacklists that were being tossed around. I did, however, earn a personal blacklist from *National Review*'s Kevin Williamson. My editor, the genial Roger Kimball, also published Williamson, and he thought that a radio debate between the two of us would make for book sales. I'm always up for a verbal donnybrook, so I agreed. But when the time came for the debate, I called in and found myself talking to the host alone. There was some problem reaching Williamson, I was told. And so we filled up the airtime until, ten minutes later, Williamson phoned in. He explained that he had paused to consider whether he wanted to talk to someone he so despised as me. This seemed to me a stunningly effective way to score debater's points, but that was the high point, as Williamson had little more to say apart from describing the manifold ways in which I was the lowest worm that God had ever suffered to crawl upon the face of the earth.

In the end, I couldn't blame Williamson or the other NeverTrumpers. If the Republican Workers Party was to be born, it was necessary that their rigid, ideological and uncaring party should die.

CHAPTER 4

MEETINGS WITH REMARKABLE PEOPLE

During the campaign I had my own little project, promoting my latest book, *The Way Back*. In it I had argued that income immobility and the rise of an American aristocracy were the dominant issues in American politics. They elected Obama in 2012 and would elect a Republican in 2016 if he ran on them. What troubled American parents more than anything else was the thought that their children would not be as well off as they were. That was the core concern. Problems like our mediocre schools, our unhinged immigration system, our departures from the rule of law were important only insofar as fixing them would lead to a mobile, classless society. Trump would offer the same remedies as I had proposed in my book, and he went out of his way to praise it.

Trump and I had both arrived at the same conclusion, that the fundamental political issue was the betrayal of the American Dream in a newly immobile country. There was an immense gulf between us, but the wealthy developer from Queens and the kid from Saskatchewan had both been outsiders who came in from the cold, and who saw class distinctions that others had missed. We had the same ideas about education and immigration, and the evils of public corruption and crony capitalism; and we knew that addressing those problems would make us socially and economically mobile again. That's what American greatness meant to us.

Roger Kimball had published my book, and he suggested a June 2016 salon in New York to promote it. A salon, I learned, is a dinner at which an author describes his book to a small group of people. What could be nicer, I thought! And to get things started he had me meet David DesRosiers of Real Clear Politics, who would assemble the guest list.

While little known, David is one of the most important people in American politics, as he selects the articles that will appear on the Real Clear website. He's the spitting image of the late Andrew Breitbart, with the same ebullience, the same energy and the same network of friends and allies. He knows everyone who matters on the right, and if he hadn't known me before we met, that just proved that I hadn't mattered until then. But when I told him at lunch I'd be ducking out early to discuss my book with Jared Kushner, he arranged a killer salon.

Twenty people attended, upstairs at Alain Ducasse's Benoit Bistro (not quite the place to preach revolution, admittedly). They included major Trump donors, literary agents, people from the *Wall Street Journal*, the *New York Post*, the *New York Observer* and Fox News, a world I had never seen before. I found them all fascinating. I'm always happy to meet new people, and if I get to tell them about one of my books, it's very heaven. I chatted with each of them, and seemed to make a particular impression on one person, a tall, thin fellow of about forty-five. My new friend had a blog, I discovered, one he suggested I write for. It was the first time I met Michael Anton, who soon became one of my closest friends.

Anton had served in several national security positions during the George W. Bush administration. He was President Bush's foreign policy and national security speechwriter, and Condoleezza Rice's chief speechwriter when she was the national security advisor. After leaving the White House, however, he concluded that the administration's efforts at exporting democracy had been a disaster, and he particularly admired Trump's April 2016 foreign policy speech, the one that I had a hand in drafting and that supplied many of the core ideas of the administration's national security strategy.

When dinner was over, several of us repaired downstairs for drinks. I chatted with Sam Schneider from Roger's publishing house, while Anton and David DesRosiers huddled in the corner. I saw David put his hand on Anton's back, as if to comfort him, for he seemed on the point of tears. What had happened, I discovered afterward, was that he had just learned that the co-editors of his blog, the *Journal of American Greatness*, had decided to blow it up because they disapproved of Anton's support for Donald Trump.

I soon discovered that the *Journal of American Greatness* (JAG) had acquired a cult following among conservative political theorists. Inevitably, its shutdown inspired a "Hitler Downfall" parody, this one from Steve Hayward, a Reagan biographer. Here's Hitler getting the fall-of-Berlin news from his top generals:

GERMAN GENERAL 1: The polls say we're losing rapists, murderers, and the not-best people. Also women, blacks, suburbanites, urbanites, Latinos, college-educated, and K Street. And we're still opposed by Pete Wehner, Bill Kristol, and George Will.

HITLER: At least we still have the Journal of American Greatness. They'll see us through to victory in November.

GERMAN GENERAL 1: My Fuhrer...JAG...

GERMAN GENERAL 2: The Journal of American Greatness has closed down. They're saying it was all satire.

HITLER (*fumbling with glasses*): Everyone leave the room except Lewandowski, Manafort, Priebus, and Donald Jr. (*The others shuffle out.*) Now what?

GERMAN GENERAL 1: We still have Frank Buckley and the *American Spectator*.

HITLER: He's Canadian, you imbecile!...I'm not trying to make Canada great again!

JAG had been required reading for those who, like Hayward and Anton, had some connection to the Claremont Graduate School in California, or who were followers of Leo Strauss, the University of Chicago philosopher. Inexplicably, Strauss had acquired a notoriety as the thinker behind George W. Bush's foreign policy excesses. How anyone might have drawn a line from Strauss's insistence on a close reading of the classical texts of Greek philosophy to the invasion of Iraq was a bit of a mystery, and Strauss himself was apolitical. Walter Berns, a political philosopher who had been a student of Strauss, told me that his teacher had voted only once. Berns knew this because Strauss had had to ask his young student to accompany him, as he had no idea where the polling station was. And so Strauss was led to vote—where he cast a ballot for Adlai Stevenson in the 1952 election.

Anton's JAG had combined support for Trump—or "Trumpism"—with a learning worthy of Strauss himself. A natty dresser and a wit, Anton had even written a Straussian satire on men's fashion. Called *The Suit*, and modeled on Machiavelli's *The Prince*, Anton's little book explained how the Florentine philosopher's "great" might seek sartorial power in their perpetual struggle against the ill-dressed "people."[1] It was an elegant joke, but what Anton wrote for JAG, under the pseudonym of Publius Decius Mus, was highly scholarly; and his esoteric blog became the must-read site for a small group of conservative political theorists.

Anton and I stayed in close touch after the salon. I was offering my thoughts on transition matters, on how to staff the new administration, and suggested that Anton should be part of the team. What he wanted to be was assistant to the president and deputy national security advisor for strategic communications. The "anti–Ben Rhodes," as he put it. Rhodes was the *éminence grise* of the Obama foreign policy team. And in January 2017, Anton got his job.

The Trump transition team got off to a rocky start. The official co-chairs were Jared and Chris Christie, but Jared told me he was chiefly concerned to get his father-in-law elected and that he deferred to Christie on potential appointments. Before long, the dulcet New Jersey accent was heard throughout the Trump transition office.

Much has been made of the fact that Christie, as a prosecutor in 2004, had put Charles Kushner, Jared's father, in jail for illegal campaign contributions, criminal tax evasion and witness tampering. At age twenty-three, a year out of Harvard College and a first-year law student at NYU, Jared was thrust into the leadership of his father's multibillion-dollar real estate holding and development companies. Jared is very bright, but I can't begin to imagine what that must have been like. He is very close to his father, and at the Kushner Company's headquarters at 666 Fifth Avenue in New York, a few blocks from the Trump Tower where he then lived, there was a prominent picture of his father. But I never detected any sign that Jared resented Christie or bore him ill will.

When I mentioned Anton to Jared, he directed me to Christie's people. And there the matter languished. A few weeks later I reminded Jared that no one had reached out to Anton, or to the other names we had suggested. "The Jersey boys don't seem to play well with others," I told him, and he said he'd fix that. But then another problem arose to slow things down. It involved a major Trump issue: how Hillary Clinton had handled Benghazi as secretary of state.

On September 12, 2012, an Islamic radical group, Ansar al-Sharia, attacked the U.S. diplomatic compound in Benghazi and killed Ambassador Chris Stevens. In at least three ways, Clinton's fingerprints were all over the attack. First, as secretary of state she had backed the invasion of Libya that overthrew Muammar Gaddafi in 2011, so much so that the *Washington Post* called it "Hillary's War." It had been sold to the public as part of a pro-democratic "Arab Spring" uprising against Middle East dictators, but it had replaced allies such as Egypt's Hosni Mubarak and defanged leaders such as Gaddafi with Islamic radicals. In Egypt this was the Muslim Brotherhood, and in Libya it was, among others, Ansar al-Sharia. The second problem for Clinton was that she seemed asleep at the wheel when the attack began, at about 3:40 p.m. EDT (9:40 p.m. in Libya). Third, she then put out a ridiculous cover-up story, suggested by Ben Rhodes, that the attacks were a popular revolt sparked by an obscure anti-Islamic video made in California. The presidential election was two months away, and the Obama administration feared it would be embarrassed if word got out that its Middle East policies had unleashed an attack that killed an American ambassador. Shamelessly, Secretary Clinton even repeated the cover-up lie to the mother of one of the victims, and then accused the mother of lying about what she had said.

For whatever reason, congressional Republicans played down the story, and that became a problem in staffing the new administration. Mike Rogers (R-MI) had chaired the House Intelligence Committee in 2014 when it issued a report that all but absolved Secretary Clinton from any responsibility for the Benghazi attack. Then Rogers retired abruptly, choosing not to run for re-election in a safe Republican seat. There was speculation that he had toned down the report at the request of his wife, who was the CEO of the American branch of the firm that hired the Blue Mountain Group to provide security at Benghazi. Even Speaker John Boehner had had enough of Rogers. But he was well liked by Chris Christie, and in late July 2016 the Trump campaign announced that Rogers would oversee the national security transition team.

For Trump supporters in the know, this was devastating news. All were aware that Mike Rogers had botched the Benghazi investigation, and none wanted anything to do with him. Trump had made Clinton's misdeeds on Benghazi a centerpiece of his campaign, and I told Jared that giving Rogers a prominent role in the campaign would take away the scandal as an issue. So Jared asked me what to do with Rogers and Christie. Reassign them or get rid of them, I told him. But he had a better idea. Why make enemies in the middle of the campaign? So they continued to hold themselves out as heads of the transition team, and their staffers continued to ask for résumés, while their jobs were very quietly given to others. Right after the election they were told that they were dismissed, though in reality they had been fired three months before. It's just that no one had informed them, and all the résumés they had received gathered dust. That was one reason for the chaos when the new administration took over.

Jared asked me to propose several possible replacements for Rogers. I knew that Trump was very sensitive about the criticism he had received from Republican foreign policy mandarins. Many of them had signed a letter before the election announcing that they wouldn't vote for him. And so I restricted the search to people who hadn't signed the letter. But even that didn't suffice. I admired Elliott Abrams, one of the smartest people in the Bush 43 White House, and someone who now thought better of nation building in Iraq. Anton and I hoped there would be a place for him in the State Department, but it was not to be. He had had a good interview with Trump, but thereafter another friend of mine assembled a list of everything Abrams had said that was mildly critical of Trump and passed it on to Steve Bannon. That was enough to doom Abrams.

After talking it over with Anton, I suggested Mike Flynn and John Bolton. Obama had made Flynn his director of the Defense Intelligence Agency, and Trump had appointed him to his do-nothing board of foreign policy advisors and briefly considered him as his running mate. And so we thought he had been vetted and knew he would survive Trump's scrutiny.

I had known a few things about Flynn. But in truth I knew no more about him than any of us had known about Obama in 2008!

We later learned that Flynn had been paid $33,000 by the RT television network to attend a dinner in Moscow, where he sat next to Vladimir Putin. RT is a Russian propaganda outlet that has since been required to register as a foreign agent in the United States. It didn't smell good, but you'd be surprised at how many Washington insiders have taken foreign moneys or accepted questionable foreign junkets.

We also knew nothing about Flynn's dealings with the Turks. He had not registered as a foreign agent of the Turkish government, but probably should have—like Tony Podesta. On Election Day, Flynn published a troubling op-ed in *The Hill*, one long smear of Fethullah Gülen,[2] a Turkish national living in the United States and the head of a large charter school movement in this country. Gülen wouldn't be of great interest but for the fact that he's a political opponent of Recep Tayyip Erdoğan, the Turkish president, whose government has asked that Gülen be extradited to Turkey. The Turkish government is demented on the subject of Gülen, as I have seen up close. On the two occasions when I appeared on the national Turkish television network I was pressed about whether the U.S. would extradite him. Obama had very properly brushed aside the request, but Flynn's op-ed signaled that the new administration might, shamefully, accede to it. Five months after the op-ed appeared, Flynn revealed that he had been paid a half million dollars by a Turkish businessman with ties to Erdoğan, and that the businessman had vetted the piece. Flynn hadn't told *The Hill* anything of this, and the campaign certainly didn't know about it.

Flynn has subsequently been pilloried for a pre-inauguration phone call with the Russian ambassador. The call violated the Logan Act, which criminalizes discussions between private citizens and foreign governments with the intent to influence another country's dealings with the United States. No one has ever been convicted of a Logan Act offense, however, and the last time anyone was charged under the statute was in 1803. Nor was there anything surprising about a president-elect asking his people to talk to foreign leaders in the stump period before the inauguration, as Obama is reported to have done with Iranian officials in 2008. The problem was that Flynn lied to the FBI about the phone call, which was enough for a criminal charge and a guilty plea. Had he told the truth, he wouldn't have been charged.

John Bolton, on the other hand, wasn't under any legal clouds. He also hadn't signed any anti-Trump letters, and is one of the smartest foreign policy experts around. I thought him impetuous, injudicious and ill-tempered, but Anton was his warm supporter. We knew that Bolton had been an architect of the 2003 invasion of Iraq, but Anton assured me that Bolton recognized that the subsequent effort at nation building had been folly. And so we recommended him. His ties to the Bush 43 White House were enough to rule him out, but that mistake was corrected in March 2018 when he replaced H. R. McMaster as national security advisor. As if to confirm all my concerns about Bolton, however, one of his first acts was to fire Anton, who had been his chief booster. In Washington, few good deeds go unpunished.

Back in the summer of 2016, I had been pushing for Anton's appointment to the national security team, but without much effect. August was a quiet month in the campaign, and he was off on holiday in California. When I reached out to him mid-month, he told me he was crankier than usual. And then on September 5 he sent me a link to an article he had just published in the *Claremont Review*. "There's a bit of fight left in me," he added.

The article was titled "The Flight 93 Election," and it's been described as the most consequential piece of American political writing since Thomas Paine's *Common Sense* in 1776.

CHAPTER 5

DECLINE

When Islamic jihadists commandeered United Flight 93 on September 11, 2009, they were aiming to hit the U.S. Capitol. Two hijacked planes had already plowed into the World Trade Center, and a third had struck the Pentagon. The fourth one, Flight 93, never reached its target. Passengers knew the plane had been hijacked, and in phone calls to loved ones they learned that they were destined for death. They understood that they would probably be killed if they fought the hijackers, but that they would certainly die if they didn't. They all died in the end, but not before the heroic passengers stormed the cockpit and brought the plane down in a field near Shanksville, Pennsylvania.

America is on Flight 93, said Michael Anton. If we do nothing, we'll all die. Our only chance is to resist and storm the cockpit, which means dislodging a corrupt establishment and electing Trump. It probably won't happen, and we'll probably die anyway. But that's our only chance. "Trump, alone among candidates for high office in this or in the last seven (at least) cycles, has stood up to say: I want to live. I want my party to live. I want my people to live. I want to end the insanity." The impassioned call to action sounded much like the decision of another intellectual who saw a crisis of history and made a choice "against death and for life." That was how Whittaker Chambers described his decision to become a communist in 1925 (one that, of course, he later reversed).[1]

Anton's essay was a sensation. Rush Limbaugh spent two days reading it to his listeners, while virtually every pundit, right and left, ridiculed it. Hillary Clinton wasn't a jihadist, they pointed out, and we weren't all going to die. The descent had been to corruption and mediocrity, and while that's bad enough, Anton had greatly overstated things. All true, but then so too had Thomas Paine in *Common Sense*, not to mention Whittaker Chambers. A pamphlet's success often depends less upon its accuracy than upon the deeper truths it reveals. The deeper truth behind Anton's essay was that America was no longer as great as we had thought.

SHADOWLANDS

I keep my sanity by not watching television, but I do watch YouTube, dog vids and all. And occasionally there's a clip that almost makes me wish I had a TV. One of these is the teaser from the HBO series *The Newsroom*, featuring Jeff Daniels as Will McAvoy, a TV anchor who prizes his objectivity and tries to remain politically neutral. Seated between a flaming liberal and a Ted Cruzbot right-winger, McAvoy is asked by a young blond student why he thinks America is the greatest country. He dodges the question, but when pressed he finally shocks everyone with his answer.

> It's not the greatest country in the world! ... [To the right-winger:] With a straight face you're going to tell students that America is so star-spangled awesome that we're the only ones in the world that have freedom? CANADA has freedom. Japan has freedom. The UK, France, Italy, Germany, Spain, Australia, BELGIUM has freedom!
>
> And you, sorority girl, just in case you accidentally walk into a voting booth some day, there are some things you should know, and one of them is, there is absolutely no evidence to support the statement that we are the greatest country in the world. We're seventh in literacy, 27th in math, 22nd in science, 49th in life expectancy, 178th in infant mortality, third in median household income, number four in labor force and number four in exports.
>
> None of this is the fault of a 20-year-old college student, but you, nonetheless, are without a doubt a member of the worst-period-generation-period-ever-period, so when you ask what makes us the greatest country in the world, [shouting] I don't even know what the f*** you're talking about! Yosemite?

If that's where we were in 2012 when the show aired, it's only gotten worse since then. According to the Program for International Student Assessment (PISA) tests administered by the Organization for Economic Cooperation and Development, in 2015 our high school students ranked 24th in reading, 38th in math and 25th in science among First World students. In our K–12 public schools, we're an honorary member of the Third World. Nevertheless, McAvoy's little diatribe was so distressing that the show attributed it to a psychotic episode. Americans don't talk like that unless they've gone off the deep end.

The problem is that Will McAvoy expressed what we increasingly think. We've told pollsters that we're on the wrong track (64 to 29 percent), and that our children will have it worse than we did (50 to 23 percent). We believe there are different rules for the well connected and people with money (83 to 10 percent).[2] American greatness, which once looked so obvious, has seemed to fade.

We've come face to face with what a hundred years ago Oswald Spengler called *Der Untergang des Abendlandes*. That's usually translated as "The Decline of the West," but I prefer the more poetic "The Going Down of the Shadowlands." The Enlightenment's sunny confidence has dimmed, and so too the nineteenth century's clear-sighted materialism. We placed our faith in the prophets of modernity, whose lights are now obscured, and today we live in their shadows.

That is what Anton told us. We were no longer great, and would never be great unless we fought back and, taking our last desperate chance, elected the man who promised to Make America Great Again.

DID WE REALLY DECLINE?

How different it all was not so very long ago. In 1945 a triumphant America produced half of the world's gross domestic product. Europe was emerging from a devastating war, one that had impoverished Britain and France and Germany, and Japan lay prostrate at our feet. China was emerging from an eight-year conflict with Japan, and would shortly be riven by a civil war that would end with the defeat of Chiang Kai-shek at the hands of Communist forces. South America was hobbled by dictatorships and growth-killing ideologies.

American dominance didn't last. Europe rebounded over the next thirty years, a period the French called the *trente glorieuses*. Between 1950 and 1970, France's annual GDP growth rate was a remarkable 4 percent, according to Thomas Piketty.[3] In the 1990s the Soviet Union broke up, and several of its former client states liberalized their economies. The Asian Tigers embraced free-market principles and very quickly became highly prosperous. China adopted a form of authoritarian capitalism that brought 700 million people out of extreme poverty, a feat unmatched in world history.

As other countries became richer, America's share of world GDP fell to 22 percent. What we experienced was *relative* decline, and it's expected to continue. The Conference Board predicts that China's share of world GDP will soon surpass that of the United States.

Ninety years ago, Ernest Hemingway could live cheaply in Paris, but things are different today. Lunch at the Brasserie Lipp, a Hemingway favorite, is now $30, which is more than what most Washington D.C. restaurants charge. At the Café Flore across the street, where Jean-Paul Sartre sat out the Occupation and wrote *Being and Nothingness*, the coffee is $8. Meanwhile, a ton of tourists from foreign countries now come to America with money to spend, and some behave with the same bad manners for which we used to be criticized when we went abroad. It won't be long before they start taking our photos and calling us quaint.

In *absolute* terms we haven't fallen behind. We're far wealthier than we were in 1945, or even in 1970. Along with our increased purchasing power, we have new technologically driven consumer products—home computers, cell phones, life-saving drugs—that were unavailable or unaffordable in the very recent past. A person with a modest salary today lives far better than an eighteenth-century aristocrat in material terms.

What happened wasn't the "decline of the West" so much as the "rise of the rest." We declined, relative to other countries, because they had gotten ahead. They had abandoned socialist planning and dictatorial government, and mimicked our free-market and democratic principles; and that was just what we had wanted them to do. And still want. As for the 700 million people (about a tenth of the world's population) who still live on less than a dollar a day, in countries such as Zimbabwe and Haiti, we'd want to see them freer and richer even if it means a further decline in the U.S. share of world GDP.

And yet we're still uneasy about the relative decline. There are two nagging doubts. First, we fear that what's happening is not just other countries playing catch-up. Perhaps we're not as entrepreneurial as we used to be. We've spawned a wasteful regulatory state and an inefficient crony capitalism that transfers wealth from politically unconnected to politically connected firms. If other countries are growing their economies faster, maybe it's because they are freer.

Second, we're uneasy because we *do* measure our own well-being against that of others. I might be made better off if my employer gives me a $100 bonus, but if everyone else at work got $10,000, I'll be unhappy about the $100. We inevitably judge our situation comparatively and relative to others, and that's true of whole countries as well. It's why Americans aren't entirely comfortable with the thought that other countries have surpassed us.

The comparison with other countries matters even more when we think of our children and grandchildren. Consider our economy's growth rate: between 1948 and 2000, the U.S. GDP grew at a 2.3 percent annual rate, which isn't horrible, but from 2000 to today it's been less than 1 percent annually.[4] By contrast, China experienced about 10 percent annual growth from 2000 to 2016, and never less than 7 percent. If the 7 percent annual growth were to continue over the next century, the Chinese economy would increase by a factor of more than 800. If the U.S. growth rate continued at 2 percent during that time, we would have only a sevenfold increase in a century, while 1 percent growth would yield a threefold increase—and our military footprint would shrink to Lilliputian levels.[5] As Robert Cooter and Aaron Edlin conclude, "differences in sustained growth cause one country's wealth to overtake another country faster than the mind can grasp."[6]

None of these statistics figured in Anton's "Flight 93 Election," however. His concern wasn't that other countries would overtake us, or that America was descending into mediocrity on a growth rate of 1 or 2 percent. Instead, he asked how the wealth gains of the last twenty years had been split between upper and lower classes. "How have the last two decades worked out for you, personally?" he asked. "If you're a member or fellow-traveler of the Davos class, chances are pretty well." By "Davos class" he meant not only the global elites who attend the World Economic Forum in Davos, Switzerland, but also their cosmopolitan fellow-travelers, people who holiday in Orvieto rather than Orlando, Bali rather than Branson, the members of the New Class who don't know anyone in our bottom 90 percent or much care about them either.

What Anton had said—though he hadn't fully realized it—was that a specter was haunting America. The specter of class struggle.

CHAPTER 6

WHERE DID THE DREAM GO?

My teacher was Raymond Klibansky, the long-haired medievalist. His teacher was Ferdinand Tönnies, who taught us the difference between *Gemeineschaft* (solidarity) and *Gesellschaft* (statecraft). *His* mentor was Friedrich Engels. So there are only three generations between you, gentle reader, and the *Communist Manifesto*.

With all the horrors of communism, with all the misery it unleashed on the world, Karl Marx still has something to tell us, something about the problem he had with America. It didn't fit with his theories. He said that society progressed in stages: first feudalism, then capitalism, then socialism. But in 1852, when he wrote *The Eighteenth Brumaire of Louis Napoleon*, the most advanced capitalist society was that of the United States, and it was nowhere near socialism. That was a bit of an embarrassment for Marx, but he had an explanation for what he might have called American Exceptionalism. There were social classes in America, but no class consciousness because the country was so mobile, he said. "True enough, the classes already exist, but [they] have not yet acquired permanent character, [and] are in constant flux and reflux, constantly changing their elements and yielding them up to one another."[1]

Throughout the twentieth century, this was the answer that sociologists, such as my late colleague Marty Lipset, gave to the question "Why didn't it happen here?"[2] Income mobility explained why we didn't have a Labor Party, as Britain did, and why socialism never took hold in the U.S. But America today is both unequal and immobile; and as this becomes more apparent, we begin to see the signs of the class consciousness and class struggle that Marx had expected. It was what the Occupy Wall Street movement and the "One Percent" protests in 2011 were all about, and the 2012 election too. It was how Bernie Sanders rose from obscurity in 2016 to challenge Hillary Clinton, whom the party establishment had backed. And it was how Donald Trump won the presidency.

On the right, about the worst thing you can call anyone is a "class warrior." What's generally meant by that is a Democrat who wants to raise taxes on the super-rich. Now, Trump supporters aren't entirely sure that that's a terrible idea. But more to the point, when the upper class is composed of liberals who support socialist measures to keep us immobile and preserve their privileged position, class warfare to free up our economy by tearing down an aristocracy is conservative and just, as well as popular. If that makes one a class warrior, maybe it isn't such a bad thing to be after all.

FATHERS AND SONS

The little town of Osawatomie, Kansas (pop. 4,300) has a special place in American history. It's where "Osawatomie" John Brown fought a pitched battle against pro-slavery forces in 1856, and it's where T. R. Roosevelt gave his "New Nationalism" speech in 1910 in honor of John Brown. Roosevelt spoke of the "conflict between the men who possess more than they have earned and the men who have earned more than they possess," and condemned what we now call crony capitalism. Osawatomie is also where, just over a hundred years later, Obama launched his re-election campaign.

He began by invoking Roosevelt's vision for a country in which "each man shall be guaranteed the opportunity to show the best that there is in him." America's grand bargain was that those who contribute to the country should share in its wealth. That bargain had made the country great, the envy of the world, but now it was betrayed by the "breathtaking greed" of the super-rich, Obama said.

> Look at the statistics. In the last few decades, the average income of the top 1 percent has gone up by more than 250 percent to $1.2 million per year.... And yet, over the last decade the incomes of most Americans have actually fallen by about 6 percent.

Inequality was the major issue in the 2012 election, and in the following year Thomas Piketty's tome on the economic divide, *Capital in the Twenty-First Century*, became a publishing sensation. We had known that the rich were getting richer and the poor poorer, but what caught our attention was Piketty's claim that over time we would necessarily become more unequal still. We soon learned, however, that Piketty had wildly overstated things, and that he didn't know much about the United States. The evidence just wasn't there.[3] But in recent years we have indeed become more economically unequal, and socially unequal too.

Between 1946 and 1980, the bottom 50 percent doubled their income (inflation-adjusted and pre-tax), but since then the trend has flatlined. By contrast, the top 10 percent—the New Class—have continued doing well, doubling their income since 1980, even after taxes. (See Appendix 1.) Gains in *wealth* were also unequal, so that by 2013, families in the top 10 percent held 76 percent of all family wealth, while those in the bottom half held just 1 percent.[4]

Many people are troubled by the growing inequalities, but the greater issue is intergenerational immobility. There's still a lot of *intra*-generational mobility (mobility during our lifetimes), in which people are born poor and die rich. Older Americans are sometimes surprised to find that they'll die as millionaires, given the way they've salted away retirement funds in houses and pension plans.[5] But even if we personally move up the ladder during our lifetime, we'll still be unhappy if we think our children won't have it as good as we did.

Economic immobility from one generation to another is not a very recent phenomenon. The likelihood of an individual child moving up from his parents' earnings bracket hasn't changed in the last twenty years, and recent scholarship tells us there hasn't been much change since 1980.[6] The change took place just before then. For children born in 1940, the rate of absolute mobility—children earning more than their parents—was 92 percent, but for children born in the 1980s the rate had fallen to 50 percent.[7] Something has happened since then to suppress mobility. Somehow, we've stopped passing on good jobs to our children.

More than anything else, this explains the rise of the Republican Workers Party: the worry that our children won't fare as well as we ourselves did, and the sense that the whole system has become unfair, that it privileges the few over the many. It isn't that we resent the basketball players and Hollywood stars in the top 0.01 percent. We willingly made them rich because we enjoyed watching them. Somehow we sense what Raj Chetty and his colleagues found when they looked at income immobility in relation to the share of the economy held by the top 1 percent: there was no relation between the two.[8] Most of us understand that the super-rich didn't make us poor, but we feel differently about the rest of the top 10 percent, the members of the New Class who have unjustly shaped the rules to produce an American aristocracy.

We don't like being on the bottom rung ourselves, but it becomes tolerable when our children have a chance to rise. That's what brought immigrants such as my ancestors to North America in the first place. Many of them knew that they'd likely fare no better in the New World than in the Old, but they expected their children to thrive. But what if they hadn't believed this? What if they had thought their children might revert to the misery of their grandparents in the old country? They would have given up.

We're hardwired to think like that. Through impulses scarcely realized, we seek to pass on our genes, and do so by having children. They will have children too, and that magnifies the forward-looking instinct to care about our descendants. The evolutionary biologist W. D. Hamilton called this the "gene's eye view" of things, and Richard Dawkins subsequently labeled it the *selfish gene* hypothesis.[9] So regarded, the gene is the decision-making principal, and the individual whose body it inhabits is merely its agent. The gene will then command the individual to perpetuate the gene's life by generating copies of itself, and that will bias us to care about our descendants and near relatives.

This explains why the social contract is front-end loaded, why family duties are paid forward. We take from our parents, and without repaying them we give to our children, and this tripartite contract is repeated across all generations. We read stories about parents who lost their lives trying to save their children from a fire, who died shielding their kids from a massacre, and we marvel at their self-sacrifice. But it's how we're programmed to behave. And that explains why immobility matters more to us than inequality.

Only three things will last to the end of time: God's promise to Abraham; the Church; and the selfish gene.

THE DREAM MOVES NORTH

Mobility was Marx's explanation for the absence of American class consciousness. In 1852, Americans thought they could get ahead, that their children would have it better than they did. But it's not 1852 anymore. As Appendix 2 shows, America today is nearly as immobile—and aristocratic—as Great Britain.

What's fascinating is how we compare with Canada, the country we most closely resemble, as illustrated in Appendix 3. Our northern neighbor is almost as mobile as uber-mobile Denmark, and far more mobile than the U.S. The differences between the U.S. and Canada are especially huge for parents in both the bottom and the top 10 percent.

For fathers in the bottom 10 percent in the U.S., there's a 57 percent chance their sons will be stuck in the bottom 10 or 20 percent of their generation. In Canada it's more like 30 percent, and the sons have a pretty good shot at making it up to the top 10 or 20 percent. There's a similar story for parents in the top 10 percent: for Americans, there's a 46 percent chance that their sons will be in the top 10 or 20 percent, while for Canadians it's a 31 percent chance. Even more stunning, Canadian kids of top 10 percent fathers have a pretty high chance of ending up in the bottom 10 percent of their cohort. Mobility works both ways, upward and downward, but in America one doesn't see much downward mobility for children of top 10 percent fathers.

The American Dream isn't dead; it just migrated to Canada, and to other countries that are more mobile than us. In what we wrongly take to be the land of opportunity, a bicoastal aristocracy, smug, self-congratulatory and disdainful of the Trump deplorables in the heartland, has cleaved itself off. Because of this we are living in what Marxists call an objectively revolutionary society.

When people said it could never happen here, they meant that a socialist revolution can't happen in a highly mobile country like America. But America isn't a mobile country anymore, and the establishments in both parties didn't see the problem. It took Trump's election to bring the issue to the fore, and even now almost no one gets it. No one understands the Republican Workers Party.

II

WHAT IS THE REPUBLICAN WORKERS PARTY?

Hast thou seen a man swift in his work?
He shall stand before kings.

Proverbs 22:29

CHAPTER 7

TWO-DIMENSIONAL MAN

Trump voters went to the polls in November 2016 determined to restore the American Dream. It's what the "Make America Great Again" slogan meant to them. They knew that our society had become immobile and that Trump had made it his issue. They saw how they had fallen behind in an economy whose gains went primarily to those at the top of the heap. But they were something more than rational economic calculators.

In a modern, market-based economy, economic immobility also means social immobility. It means that those left behind in economic terms won't be regarded as worthy of society's respect, and they'll likely be all too aware of it. When the overclass late-night comics and actors mocked them, the underclass took notice. When NeverTrumpers told them they had brought their misery on themselves through their foul habits, they filed this away. When Hillary Clinton called them deplorable, they paid attention. When their cherished institutions, their religion, their patriotism, their local loyalties were derided, they voted for Donald Trump.

The American Dream was about something more than money. It was also about individual self-worth, about the respect owed to the least of us. "A Man's a Man for a' that," sang Robert Burns. That's something the Left used to understand, as we saw in plays such as *Death of a Salesman*. The overclass forgot this, but the underclass remembered it. They were two-dimensional voters in what had become a one-dimensional Republican Party.

HOW THE REPUBLICAN WORKERS PARTY
OCCUPIES THE SWEET SPOT

In a naive view of American politics, voter preferences and political parties can all be ranged along a left-right axis defined by economics. Every voter and every politician may be pegged somewhere along the line from socialism and pure paternalism at the extreme left, to unrestrained free markets and free choices at the extreme right. That makes public policy a bloodless, technical exercise in which noneconomic preferences are suppressed. Yet those questions influence how we vote as much as or more than purely economic ones.

That's something Herbert Marcuse recognized in *One-Dimensional Man*,[1] the book that became the New Left's bible in the 1960s. Before then, the older Marxists had seen economics as the single driving force behind human history. But Soviet communism had proven repressive, and '60s leftists weren't going to take their inspiration from the aged Leonid Brezhnev or Alexei Kosygin. Instead, they turned to Marcuse, who told them that socialism had hit a brick wall, that capitalism had been able to resist the logic of Marxist dialectics by constraining economic options along a one-dimensional parameter. Consumers were free to choose, but only after their personal desires and political choices had been manipulated by mass culture and ideology, in the manner suggested by John Kenneth Galbraith. For progressives, said Marcuse, the way out was an authentic liberalization in which people recognized their bondage to an irrational technological and economic system, and sought a transformative change along a second dimension of choice. In place of one-dimensional economism, Marcuse proposed a vision of expanded possibilities that recognized everyone's essential dignity.

Before Trump, the Republican establishment had also seen politics along a single left-right economic divide. Their Democratic opponents were socialists, while they were the right-wing growth party. That was what Romney saw as his ticket to victory, in his 59-point plan full of sensible free-market ideas, a manifesto for Republican insiders which no one but them ever read. And we know where that got them. In the 2012 election the Republican one-dimensional man was left in the dustbin.

In Trump's America there's obviously more going on than a single economic axis could capture. Along a different axis, voters can be divided according to their views about a variety of other issues: nationalism versus globalism, immigration restrictions versus open borders, religion versus irreligion, and a classless versus a class society. Grouping all such concerns together, our politics can be portrayed along two axes, economic and noneconomic, according to the preferences of two-dimensional men who vote for two-dimensional parties.

That's how Lee Drutman at the Voter Survey Group saw things, in a fascinating analysis of voter preferences conducted after the 2016 general election. The questionnaire asked voters to identify both whom they voted for and how they felt about various economic and social issues. Drutman then mapped the responses in a diagram, red dots for a Trump voter, blue for Hillary Clinton, yellow for other candidates. Economic preferences were portrayed on the horizontal axis, left-wing on the left and right-wing on the right. Social preferences were shown on the vertical axis, left-wing at the bottom and right-wing at the top.

The diagram divided voters into four quadrants. The 44.6 percent who fell into the lower-left quadrant were strongly left-wing on both economic and social issues. Some of them voted for the Green Party candidate, Jill Stein, while some even voted for Trump, but more than four-fifths voted for Hillary Clinton. Next, the antipodean upper-right quadrant was composed of conservatives who were both socially and economically right-wing. They constituted 22.7 percent of all voters, and nine-tenths of them voted for Trump. A miniscule 3.8 percent of the voters were libertarians in the lower-right quadrant, socially left-wing and economically right-wing, and they split their votes evenly between Trump and Clinton. Finally, 28.9 percent of the voters occupied the upper-left quadrant, economically left-wing but socially right-wing. Drutman called them "populists," but I prefer the label that Trump himself gave them: the Republican Workers Party. They went three to one for Trump.

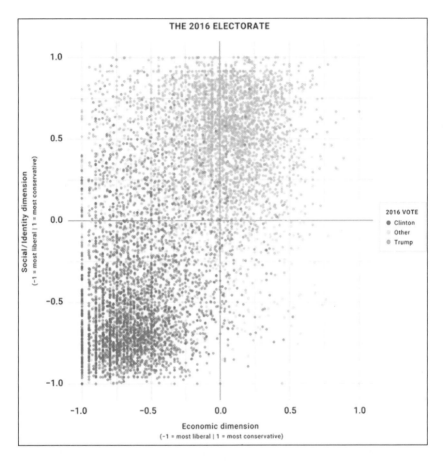

The Four Quadrants of American Politics

Source: Lee Drutman, "Political Divisions in 2016 and Beyond: Tensions Between and Within the Two Parties," Voter Survey Group, June 2017.

The Republican Workers Party in the upper-left quadrant is the winning coalition in American politics. It is liberal on economics, like the overwhelming majority of Americans (73.5 versus 26.5 percent). It's also conservative on social issues, like the majority of Americans (51.6 versus 48.4 percent). Its supporters are nationalists who feel a bond of solidarity with fellow Americans and who for that reason support liberal welfare policies. It's the sweet spot in American politics, the place where presidential elections are won, and the winner is going to be the fellow who won't touch Social Security and who promises to nominate a judge in the mold of Antonin Scalia. Donald Trump, in other words.

It turns out that Republican and Democratic voters mostly agree about economic issues. They both want to preserve Social Security and Medicare, and think that bad foreign trade agreements have led to American job losses. They disagree about the need for government intervention in the economy, but both worry about political corruption. Where they really differ is over social concerns such as immigration and moral issues such as abortion. That's the real dividing line between the parties.

After the election, bitter NeverTrumpers claimed that their favored candidate—Ted Cruz for most of them—would also have beaten Clinton. Drutman's diagram shows just what a pipe dream that is. A candidate who defines himself primarily through economic right-wing policies, whose principal concern is the country's gross domestic product, who doesn't care how wealth gains are divided among the various classes, begins with nearly three-quarters of the electorate in the other camp, and isn't going to go very far.

Sadly, right-wing intellectuals never noticed this. Too many of them are libertarians and occupy the near-empty lower-right quadrant of the social liberals and economic conservatives, the polar opposites of the Trump voters in the upper-left quadrant. The best of them, the scholars at the Cato Institute, the writers for *Reason* magazine, recognize their political impotence and joke about how they've never voted Republican. They're simply content to advance ideas in which they believe. But then there are the establishment types and the donors who describe themselves as "fiscal conservatives and social liberals." Left-wingers accord them a measure of respect, for they're thought to be on the right side of history where it matters (same-sex marriage, abortion), while their inconvenient and politically improbable free-market views about the economy can be ignored. They make a lot of noise, but they're an army of generals without any troops behind them.[2] In Republican politics they're simply a costly distraction—albeit one with very deep pockets.

HOW THE DEMOCRATS ENDED UP IN THE LOSER QUADRANT

The Democrats won the popular vote in 2016, and tried to pretend that this made Trump an illegitimate president. They complained that Trump had colluded with the Russian government to tilt the election, when it was they who had paid for salacious opposition research with Russian thumbprints all over it—the infamous Steele dossier. And who could blame them? The tales of prostitutes and urine-soaked beds: what a goldmine for Hillary Clinton's campaign! Never mind where it came from. But what if, just suppose, the incredible stories were not very . . . credible? What if, instead, they were simply a useful hook on which to hang a full-scale investigation of the Trump campaign? In any event, the file somehow ended up in the hands of the FBI, whose anti-Trump partisans pounced on it, like a tiger on its prey, and seemingly used it to obtain a court order to wiretap Republican campaign workers, whose identities were then unmasked and whose campaign strategies were presumably revealed to Obama officials. The same FBI agents had also watered down key findings in the Hillary Clinton email probe to ensure that she wouldn't be charged with a criminal offense. All of this is under investigation by Congress and the Justice Department's inspector general, and a year later we seem to be left with two possibilities. Either the Trump campaign colluded with the Russians, or else the Democrats connived (and perhaps colluded) with the Russians and used all the tools at the Obama administration's command to spy on a Republican challenger in the midst of a presidential campaign—and thus far we've seen no evidence of Republican collusion.

We've since learned that Russian trolls meddled in the 2016 campaign, mostly to help Trump. In monetary terms it was small potatoes. And if they had wanted to disrupt our politics, it's unlikely they could have done very much. We're already at peak craziness. Was it the Russians who prompted Senator Tim Kaine to call for progressives to fight in the streets? Did the Kremlin edit the *Washington Post*? We don't need the Russians to make a mockery of American politics. We do it all by ourselves.

After a while, it all got boring. After a while, nothing was new. We didn't have to listen to what was said, since we knew it all yesterday. It wasn't that we were peddled fake news. It wasn't even news, for news is about new things. Newspapers don't have to tell us the sun rose this morning, that water is wet, that they despise Trump. We know all that.

The stories went nowhere, and the Democrats know they're in a bind. They want to learn how to connect with the forgotten voter in the heartland. Drutman's little diagram tells them how they can do so. And also why they can't. We know they're outraged about losing the election, but that's all they've got. So far they haven't come up with winning policies. Centered so low on the vertical axis on social issues, they can't walk away from progressive identity politics, from full abortion rights, from Black Lives Matter, from "gender identity." They're stuck in the loser quadrant.

If Democrats are ever to emerge from it, one of two things must happen. The first is a revival of the social conservatism of an older Democratic Party, the party of Tip O'Neill and Daniel Patrick Moynihan. That's what some astute Democrats—people such as Thomas Frank, Mark Lilla and Van Jones—are now suggesting. Focus on economic issues, not social ones, they say. Their party had ridiculed Trump's socially conservative voters, who surprisingly had noticed. But before the Democrats can embrace social conservatism, the party's entire leadership must pass away, to be replaced by a new generation, and that won't happen anytime soon.

The second way out for Democrats is what John Keble, the nineteenth-century Anglican divine, called national apostasy. In America, this would mean the abandonment by Americans of their social conservatism, their religious traditions. Instead, they would adopt the Democrats' social liberalism, as preached by our media and force-fed to students at our schools and universities.

That was how the Democrats approached the 2016 election. It was Herbert Butterfield's "Whig theory of history" dressed up as a campaign strategy.[3] The party assumed that the arc of history, to which Obama so frequently appealed, bent only their way and that, in the fullness of time, the country would fall into their laps. All of history moved, not without a few bumps to be sure, in their direction; and everything that went before had been merely a preparation, a prologue, for its apotheosis in the persons of Obama and Hillary Clinton. With that thought in mind, there was no reason to court the deplorables, with their retrograde beliefs about religion and morality, as they would inevitably fall into line, coaxed along by gentle nudges from late-night comedy shows, diversity officers and the Civil Rights division of the Department of Education.

It wasn't an idle fantasy. According to the Voter Survey Group, we're just barely a social conservative country. A 2 percent swing to social liberalism would be enough to turn the tide. With their messianic fervor, the social liberals in the Democratic Party could then be expected to force their agenda down the throats of social conservatives, caring little about how divisive it might be. Lee Drutman thinks this electoral shift might happen, and it worries him; for while he's a liberal, he is also an old-fashioned patriot who would lament the fracturing of his country.

Because the Democrats are centered so low on Drutman's vertical axis, because they're so very socially liberal, I don't see national apostasy on the horizon. But were this to happen, were the social liberals to find themselves in the majority, divisiveness and oppression would be the icing on the cake for many of them, given their contempt for conservatives. Obama's solicitor general, for example, suggested that Catholic and other religious colleges that are faithful to their beliefs might lose federal funds.[4] During Senate confirmation hearings in 2017, a Democratic senator asked a judicial nominee whether she was an orthodox Catholic, while another Democratic senator worried that "the dogma lives loudly in you."[5] Hillary Clinton herself said that our legal system must change "deep-seated cultural codes, religious beliefs and structural biases," so as to ensure ready access to abortion.[6]

In the past, liberals could make their peace with conservative religious voters through what Terry Eagleton, a Marxist, calls the "double truth" thesis.[7] Under it, there is one kind of truth for the learned and a very different one for the unlearned. The eighteenth-century rationalist had abandoned religious belief, but didn't try to impose his skepticism on the lower orders, for fear of political unrest were their comforting illusions stripped away. Voltaire might courageously discuss atheism, noted Carl Becker, "but not before the servants."[8] On the right, many of the "East Coast Straussians," with their talk of esoteric learning, still subscribe to double truths, but on the left an accommodation with traditional religious belief is difficult. Modern liberalism is invasive and doesn't tolerate people with politically incorrect ideas about families and sexual behavior. The peasants in flyover country can no longer be left with their benighted beliefs. They have to be gentrified.

And that's the difference between liberals and conservatives. It's principally the former who wish to impose their beliefs on dissenters. It's the liberals who have become intolerant, who can't leave people alone, who scratch where it doesn't itch. They're quick to detect a whiff of holy fascism in the conservative agenda. But conservatives accepted gay marriage and abandoned the racial prejudices that so disfigured the Old Right. Of course black lives matter, they think, and they'll resent the insinuation that they believe otherwise. But that's not good enough for liberals, who insist that conservatives are irredeemably (*le mot* de Hillary) racist, sexist, transphobic, you name it.

The social conservative awakening that helped elect Trump came when voters realized that the liberal agenda amounted to something more than a shield to protect sexual minorities. It was also a sword to be used against social conservatives. The Trump voters might have grumbled about the 2015 Supreme Court *Obergefell* decision that recognized a right to same-sex marriage.[9] But that didn't pick anyone's pocket, and no great political protest followed. It was a different story when homosexual activists employed their newly won rights to put religious believers out of business. In a case that seemed to signal where we were headed, the labor commissioner for the state of Oregon, Brad Avakian, ordered the owners of a bakery to pay $135,000 in damages for refusing on religious grounds to make a wedding cake for a lesbian couple. Oregon law prohibits discrimination based on sexual orientation, and the bakers were told what that meant. "Within Oregon's public accommodations law," wrote Avakian, "is the basic principle of human decency that every person, regardless of their sexual orientation, has the freedom to fully participate in society." The bakers lost their business, and were labeled as bigots to boot.[10] There were plenty of other bakers around, and one of them even donated a wedding cake to the lesbian couple, but that didn't seem to matter.

Thus does liberalism turn on itself and become invasive. It didn't begin that way. "The state has no business in the bedrooms of the nation," said Pierre Elliott Trudeau fifty years ago, in proposing to decriminalize homosexuality. To all but the most intolerant, that made perfect sense. But now, the state seeks to make the nation's bedrooms its business, under the ethic of enforced "respect" for sexual minorities championed by Justice Anthony Kennedy. A headline in the *Babylon Bee*, that reliable news source, nailed it: "'Our love life is none of your business,' says couple forcing business owner to approve their love life." *A, Corydon, Corydon, quae te dementia cepit!*

The cultural Left's sexual politics gives them a twofer. It allies them to a forgotten group of voters and flips the bird at religious conservatives. Both desires animate the Left, and of the two the second is likely the stronger. It's not about sympathy so much as antipathy, not so much about defending sexual minorities as the desire to *épater les dévots*, to attack their most resolute opponent. That's why the Left so quickly moved on after winning the debate over same-sex marriage, to embrace the cause of the transgendered. So long as the ideological enemy remains, there's always one more river to cross.

In our culture wars, in Hillary's condemnation of the deplorables, the religious voter experienced a reverse Sally Fields moment: "You dislike me! You really dislike me!" And why try to win the respect of those who sincerely despise you? That had been the mistake of all the well-tamed conservatives who tried to persuade liberals just how sweetly reasonable they were. Better to provoke them by affirming your deepest beliefs.

In the eyes of the liberal elite, Catholics were especially retrograde. In 2012, New York's Cardinal Dolan offered to say a prayer at the Democratic National Convention, after he accepted a Republican invitation to do so at their convention. But the Democrats ignored the offer, fearful that a prayer by a prominent pro-life leader would anger feminists. Worse, a motion to include a reference to God in the Democratic platform was roundly booed by the delegates. God was back in at the 2016 Democratic convention, but the party platform dropped the religious liberty exemption on abortion that had been in the 2012 platform. Then Tom Perez, the chairman of the Democratic National Committee, announced that his party has no room for candidates who don't share its official position on abortion, in case there was any doubt.[11]

Democrats in the past would have been horrified to learn that their party makes faithful Catholics feel unwanted. That's what they thought Republicans did! Catholics are the principal block of swing voters in presidential elections, and with the exception of 2000 they have backed the winner in every election since 1952. They were JFK liberals and an important part of the Reagan Democrat coalition. On social issues they're conservative, but on economic issues they're liberal, faithful to the Church's social teachings about the need to remedy economic inequalities. As such, they occupy the political landscape's dead center.

While Hillary Clinton ignored Catholics, Trump went out of his way to court them. It didn't happen overnight. Early in the campaign he picked a stupid quarrel with Pope Francis. But by the end he was persuaded to grant a lengthy interview to the Catholic EWTN television network, and to tweet his happiness at the canonization of Mother Teresa. The mainstream media didn't notice any of this, but Catholics did. They were plus-seven for Trump, and white Catholics were plus-23 for him, providing him with the winning margin in the crucial rust-belt states of Pennsylvania, Ohio, Michigan and Wisconsin. And that was the election.

At a dinner party, I told all this to a *New York Times* reporter. "What's EWTN?" he asked me.

Everyone had been looking in the wrong place. The Democrats had the media, the money, the ground game and all the savvy digital gurus. They had Facebook in their back pocket. But when it was discovered that the Trump campaign had hired Cambridge Analytica for a similar data-driven exercise, it became a scandal. If the Democrats had peered into our Facebook likes, that was a sign of their invincible technical sophistication. When Republicans did the same thing, it was intrigue, cabal and corruption. Like the "dark money" of anonymous campaign contributions, what is a matter for smug self-congratulations when done by Democrats becomes an outrage when done by Republicans. Yet is there any evidence that either effort made much of a difference? Perhaps we'll never know. But it's permitted to think that what drove the Trump victory were bonds of family, community and religion of which the media and the data-mining experts had not a clue.

WHY SOCIAL CONSERVATIVES ARE ECONOMIC LIBERALS

We've been told that Republicans are extremists and Democrats are moderates. Drutman's diagram shows that the opposite is true. Democratic voters occupied the deep lower-left of the map, very liberal both economically and socially. By contrast, the Republicans were socially conservative but middle-of-the-road on economic issues. In the upper-left quadrant, Republican voters were moderately left-wing on economics. And in the upper-right quadrant, they were only moderately right-wing. In both quadrants they hugged the center axis on economic questions such as trade policy and social welfare. They weren't impressed by Paul Ryan's flirtation with Randism or by Ted Cruz's checklist of right-wing principles.

There's a reason why social conservatives don't share the libertarian's antipathy to social welfare legislation, one that explains the logic of the Republican Workers Party. Social conservatism has a gravitational pull when it comes to economics: it draws voters to middle-of-the-road or liberal policies. As a nationalist, the social conservative will have a special concern for the well-being of his fellow citizens. He's going to want some form of national health care for the poor and elderly. Second, the religious voters who make up the greatest number of social conservatives can't ignore their duties to those in need without betraying their beliefs. That's particularly true of Catholic Republican voters, given the Church's principle of solidarity and its preferential option for the poor. That translates into a duty to support political parties that won't let people die in the streets, as well as a personal duty to donate to charity.

That is why the Left's casual indifference or outright hostility to religion, while it clamors for a stronger social safety net, is self-defeating. If God is not great, if it's all a pack of lies, if we're so much wiser now, then religious duties to the poor can be ignored as well. We'd have to look elsewhere for a requirement to support universal health care, and the atheist can find plenty of reasons not to do so.

Left-wing antinationalism also dismisses the strongest of reasons to help those in need: a sense of solidarity with our neighbors. When universal health care is demanded as a right, this demand assumes a correlative duty to provide it. But such duties are not owed to foreigners. I have no obligation to support an Albanian health-care system, nor is an Albanian obligated to support American health care. The argument for universal health care that the Left ignores is that it's something a nationalist owes to his fellow citizens, rather than to everyone indiscriminately, to stranger and brother alike. Sadly, the modern Left refuses to appeal to nationalist sentiments even in demanding national health care, because it finds nothing to praise in American history. It rejects a common American culture, despises its conservative opponents and then reviles them when they object to the messy Obamacare scheme. They should have seen that one coming.

Yet if they think that we're all created equal, that we're all endowed with certain unalienable rights, that ours is a government of, by and for the people, why are they not American nationalists?

CHAPTER 8

NATIONALISM

Is nationalism an unqualified good? The globalist says it isn't. Some people think it's just one step away from Nazism. So we need to examine American nationalism more closely, and see how it differs from populism, with which it's often confused.

Populism was one of the nastiest political movements of American history. It was inevitable, therefore, that Trump would be called a populist. You should never give your opponents the right to label you, but even some of Trump's supporters have called themselves populists. They should know better. Trump is a nationalist, not a populist.

It's true that Trump, like most populists, thinks that tariff walls to keep foreign goods out of the country might help American workers. But then Abraham Lincoln and William McKinley thought so too, and they weren't populists. It's also true that, like most populists, Trump championed an underclass unjustly held back by an aristocracy of wealth. But then Karl Marx and Eugene V. Debs, the socialist union leader, thought they were doing the same thing, and they weren't populists. We must also admit that Trump, like most populists, decried the influence of money in politics. But then so did Hillary Clinton and Liz Warren, and nobody called them populists.

Here's what the accusation of populism really means. It's a smear meant to link one to people such as "Pitchfork Ben" Tillman, one of the vilest people in American political history.[1] Tillman was the governor of South Carolina from 1890 to 1894 and served as the state's representative in the U.S. Senate for the next twenty-three years. He was undoubtedly a populist—the Platonic form of populism. He was also the man who invented Jim Crow laws in his state, a person who defended lynch mobs and boasted of killing black Americans. That's why the charge of populism is a dog whistle meant to tar someone as a racist.

It's also why populism shouldn't be confused with conservative nationalism. As a conservative, Trump favors socially conservative institutions and free-market solutions to political questions. As a nationalist, he is middle-of-the-road or liberal when it comes to taking care of Americans who have fallen behind. Those who confuse nationalism with populism betray an ignorance of what nationalism has meant here and in the countries we most closely resemble.

DISHING THE WHIGS

A Republican Workers Party might sound like an unnatural union of opposites, but similar parties have had a long history in English-speaking parliamentary governments, and the only question is why it took so long for one to emerge here.

Nationalists such as Trump champion the common good against corrupt special interests, as have nationalists in Britain. Long before Trump railed against the Clinton Cash machine, long before his supporters chanted "lock her up," British Tories led by Viscount Bolingbroke (1678–1751) attacked the corrupt Whig government of Sir Robert Walpole (1721–42). As an answer to corruption, Bolingbroke proposed governance by an enlightened ruler, a "patriot king" who would stand above political parties and serve the general welfare. Such a monarch would "espouse no Party, but . . . govern like the common father of his people . . . where the head and all the members are united by one common interest, and animated by one common spirit."[2] That wouldn't leave much room for the Democrats' identity politics.

Nationalists must seek to promote the well-being of all fellow citizens, and not simply a favored few. It was nationalism that pulled the Republican Workers Party to the middle of the road on economic and social welfare issues, and it was nationalism that informed Benjamin Disraeli's liberal policies in Britain. As an MP, he opposed Sir Robert Peel's free-trade legislation, and in the process he created a new Tory party. And a year before Friedrich Engels shocked readers with his description of the wretchedness of London's East End in *The Condition*

of the Working Class in England (1845), Disraeli had written no less pas-
sionately about economic inequality.[3] Then, as the Conservative leader in
the Commons and chancellor of the exchequer, Disraeli pushed through
the Second Reform Bill of 1867, extending the franchise to all adult male
heads of households. Electoral reform was going to happen anyway,
and in stealing the issue from Gladstone's Liberals he had "dished the
Whigs."

In a speech on the bill, Disraeli described what he thought the Tory
party should be, in terms that speak to our present politics.

> I have always considered that the Tory party was the national party
> of England. It is not formed of a combination of oligarchs and phi-
> losophers who practice on the sectarian prejudices of a portion of the
> people. It is formed of all classes, from the highest to the most homely,
> and it upholds a series of institutions that are in theory, and ought to
> be in practice, an embodiment of the national requirements and the
> security of the national rights.[4]

Where Disraeli said "oligarchs," think of the New Class. For "philosophers," substitute our liberal media. For his "national party," it's the
Republican Workers Party. What Disraeli had created was a socially conservative and economically liberal Tory party. He had taken the Whigs'
issues away from them, just as Trump did in dishing the Democrats.

In seeking a parallel to the Republican Workers Party in other
countries, some have pointed to the Christian Democratic parties of
Europe, such as Helmut Kohl's in Germany or Alcide De Gasperi's in
Italy. But not one American in a thousand can tell you what they were all
about. In any case, the Republican Workers Party would never call itself
Christian, even if it strongly defends religious institutions. Instead, the
proper comparison is to the Conservative or Tory parties in Britain and
Canada, to leaders such as Disraeli, Lord Randolph Churchill (Winston's
father) and even Winston Churchill himself. They were conservative,
but because they supported generous social welfare policies they are
sometimes called Red Tories.[5] And they're the ancestors of Trump's
Republican Workers Party.

With a better understanding of history, then, one would be aware of
an honorable tradition of conservative nationalism in similar countries.

If you call them populists, you don't have a clue what you're talking about. But *Red Tories*? We remember the Tories from the Revolutionary War, and we're not Tories, still less Red Tories, even if red has become the color of Republicans in America. Nevertheless, the voters demand a generous welfare system. Reform it we might, improve it we must, but even a diehard libertarian might see the political advantage in learning to live with what cannot be changed. Better still if one sees it as a positive good, as the Republican Workers Party does.

Can we expect something like Lord Randolph Churchill's Tory Democracy from the Republican Workers Party, then? Not quite, because of differences in constitutional regimes. The separation of powers in the American Constitution has given us two or more different Republican parties: a presidential party, which today is the Republican Workers Party, but also congressional Republican parties rooted in the issues and preferences of local members. There's the Freedom Caucus composed of Tea Party members, the more moderate Main Street Partnership and whatever maverick senators were thinking this morning. It is a legal fiction to call them all members of the same political party. By contrast, a parliamentary system lacks a separation of powers, and its parties are unified around their leader in the House of Commons. A prime minister may decide that an annoying member cannot run under his party's label, which ordinarily is political death for the person so expelled.

Like a Disraeli, a Trump may run as the leader of a national party. But he can't govern like one. Because of the separation of powers, he'll have to make deals with people who politically owe him nothing, who indeed may despise him. Sometimes he'll come up blank, as he did when he let congressional Republicans try to replace Obamacare. Sometimes he'll score, as he did with tax reform. And sometimes he might have to make deals with the Democrats, on health care, for example. That would be a masterstroke worthy of Disraeli. We're the party of jobs and health care, he would tell voters. We'll leave bicycle lanes and transgender bathrooms for the Democrats.

SUSPECT NATIONALISM

Two hundred and forty years ago, America spoke itself into existence as a nation with a Declaration of Independence that proclaimed the unalienable rights of individuals and the just foundation of government. That foundation, Lincoln told us, was a government of, by and for the people. And what he meant was a government of, by and for the *American* people.

Lincoln always put America first. So too did John Adams. When he presented his credentials as the first American ambassador to Great Britain, George III observed that Adams was not thought to be especially fond of France. "I must avow to your Majesty," replied Adams, "I have no Attachments but to my own Country." To which the king replied, "An honest Man will never have any other." And nationalism was what Donald Trump pledged, in his inaugural address. "From this day forward," he announced, "a new vision will govern our land. From this moment on, it's going to be America First."

That bothered people, and one reason is because there are different kinds of nationalism, some less innocent than others. Among the former is *ethnic nationalism*, which promotes a special allegiance to one's own racial or ethnic group and excludes others. In America this might be alt-right white nationalism or the black nationalism of the Black Lives Matter movement, Ta-Nehisi Coates and Louis Farrakhan. The ethnic nationalist may assert a need to correct historical injustices, but the demand for payback can mask a more primal racial hatred.

When I lived in Quebec, a separatist government enacted meanspirited language laws to administer a psychological drubbing to the province's Anglophones. I resented it, and I wasn't going to have much use either for the ethnic nationalists in America's alt-right. Nor would Trump. In his inaugural address he said, "it is time to remember that old wisdom our soldiers will never forget: that whether we are black or brown or white, we all bleed the same red blood of patriots, we all enjoy the same glorious freedoms, and we all salute the same great American Flag."

Then there is *cultural nationalism*, where what matters is assimilation into a common culture. There's nothing wrong with celebrating American writers and artists, as Americans, but for some people cultural nationalism is also a way of excluding others, and they might have been encouraged when Trump said in Warsaw that "the West will never, ever be broken. Our values will prevail. Our people will thrive. And our civilization will triumph." And did that throw the fat into the fire! Was

Trump saying that "non-Western" Americans were somehow less than American? Our people write symphonies, said Trump. Did that mean you had to appreciate high culture with a European hue to count as one of "our people"?

At the *Atlantic*, Peter Beinart detected a thinly veiled bigotry behind the speech. Trump was talking about Christendom, he said, "a particular religious civilization that must protect itself from outsiders."[6] (Monty Python told us that nobody expects the Spanish Inquisition, but the *Atlantic* expects it daily.) Then, inevitably, Charles Blow of the *New York Times* said on CNN that talk of culture is a dog whistle for racists. If we're supposed to assimilate to an American culture, he asked, are you saying that "you need to abandon your ethnicity and become more like, you know, the kind of the white America that I'm [envisioning]."

Blow wondered whether cultural nationalism would privilege Anglo-Americans, whether conservatives were employing the idea of assimilation as a weapon against America's minorities. Some alt-right types do just that, but they miss the point. Culture is not the continuation of politics by other means. And culture can be profoundly unifying. Our music and art enable us to share transcendent emotional experiences with people who may differ from us in various ways. W.E.B. Du Bois recognized this truth: "I sit with Shakespeare, and he winces not. Across the color line I move arm in arm with Balzac and Dumas, where smiling men and welcoming women glide in gilded halls."

Western culture itself is immensely diverse and absorptive. If British culture excluded foreign elements, for example, its music would have no George Frideric Handel, its literature no Joseph Conrad, its philosophy no Ludwig Wittgenstein. Going back to our Roman heritage, what is that, asks Rémi Brague, but an appropriation of Greek philosophy and a Jewish-based religion?[7] The Western culture of which Trump spoke derives its strength from its willingness to borrow from other cultures, and this is especially true of American culture.

There isn't much room for white nationalism in American culture. For alongside baseball and apple pie, it includes Langston Hughes and Amy Tan, Tex-Mex food and Norah Jones. You can be an American if you don't enjoy them, but you might be a wee bit more American if you do. The cultural nationalist is right to say that being an American is more than subscribing to the principles in the Declaration of Independence.

A lot of people in other countries do so, and they're not American. Becoming an American requires a few more things: American citizenship, and a love for American institutions that aren't owned by a single race.

There is an American culture, and it's not a white culture or a black culture or a Mexican culture. That's why the American who sincerely hates American multiculturalism is something less than an American.

LIBERAL NATIONALISM

There's a kind of cultural nationalism built into the idea of America. But far more important is another kind of nationalism, a *liberal nationalism* based on the sacred texts of our founding. That was Lincoln's idea of American nationhood in an 1858 speech on what the Fourth of July meant.

For some, the holiday was a reminder of their ancestors' patriotism and bravery. But in 1858 half of the country was foreign-born, or the descendants of people who had lived elsewhere in 1776. It didn't matter, said Lincoln. They were still entitled to celebrate the Fourth, to call themselves Americans. And what made them so was something other than ties of blood.

> When they look through that old Declaration of Independence they find that those old men say that "We hold these truths to be self-evident, that all men are created equal," and then they feel that that moral sentiment taught in that day evidences their relation to those men, that it is the father of all moral principle in them, and that they have a right to claim it as though they were blood of the blood, and flesh of the flesh, of the men who wrote that Declaration, and so they are. That is the electric cord in that Declaration that links the hearts of Patriotic and liberty-loving men together, that will link those patriotic hearts as long as the love of freedom exists in the minds of men throughout the world.[8]

And that is how American nationalism and the American identity are understood today. In other countries, it's a matter of dynastic houses and cultural icons, but America does entirely without the former and increasingly without the latter. Instead, the focal point for nationalist and patriotic sentiments is the sense that America has a special mission to promote liberty, as promised by the Declaration of Independence and guaranteed by the Bill of Rights. These have assumed the status of what the historian Pauline Maier called "American Scripture."[9]

The Republican Workers Party is nationalist, and rejects the anti-national globalism, the open borders of the Democrats and of yesterday's Republican Party. It also embraces a distinctly American kind of nationalism. Unlike the reactionary paleocons, or the leftist Frankfurt School, the Republican Workers Party glories in the Enlightenment beliefs of our Founders. These it accepts as its own. It is faithful to the principles of the Declaration because they are American, and not only because they're pretty good ideas. American nationalism is liberal nationalism, and nothing like the ethnic tribalism of Johann Gottfried Herder or his Nazi epigones. Instead, it rests on a sense of solidarity with all Americans, rather than with the Democrats' narrower identity groups. While it's possible to be a German white nationalist, an American white nationalist is a contradiction in terms.

Trump's critics were quick to detect the whiff of fascism in his nationalism. It doesn't take a history degree to recognize how hysterical this is, but if historical perspective were needed, Jean-François Revel provided it when he observed that, while the dark night of fascism is always said to be descending on America, somehow it lands only in Europe. And that's because constitutional liberties are the icon of American nationhood and constitutive of our identities as Americans. For Americans, as Americans, illiberalism is self-defeating, and when Americans have been illiberal in the past, in time they've been seen to be un-American.

LIBERTY, EQUALITY, FRATERNITY

People wouldn't worry so much about American nationalism if they recognized that it is necessarily liberal. That became clear in the Supreme Court's *Texas v. Johnson* decision to protect political protests that take the form of flag burning. The Stars and Stripes is an icon of nationhood, but not so fundamental as the constitutional right of free speech. When courts uphold, on free speech grounds, the rights of protesters to burn an American flag, they're not trivializing a national symbol; instead, they prefer an abstract fundamental icon—the Bill of Rights—to a less central symbol—the flag. "If there is a bedrock principle underlying the First Amendment," ruled the Court, "it is that the government may not prohibit the expression of an idea simply because society finds the idea itself offensive or disagreeable."[10]

At the same time, nationalism can't be employed to divide one group of Americans from another. American nationalism must be egalitarian, and a nationalism that makes second-class citizens of some Americans, based upon their race or sexual orientation, is profoundly anti-American. But neither should the Bill of Rights, an icon of American nationalism, be employed to marginalize people on the basis of their political or religious beliefs. In other words, not every political issue should be turned into a constitutional one, in a way that only divides us further.

In politics there are always winners and losers, and there is nothing particularly dishonorable about being on the losing side of a political debate. In constitutional debates, however, the loser's argument is judged to be fundamentally illegitimate. Because constitutional rights are at the heart of our national identity, taking the wrong side on a constitutional question comes to be seen as un-American. The baker who refuses to provide a wedding cake for a gay couple is not just labeled a bigot and dragged into court, which is bad enough. He'll also be branded un-American if he's judged to have trenched on constitutionally protected rights. Today people sneer at the House Un-American Affairs Committee of the 1950s, at the very idea of calling people "un-American" for their politics. Yet this lives on in litigation meant to show that the many millions of religiously conservative Americans are less than American, even if they do no harm to others. And that's unnecessarily divisive.

Nationalism also has something to say about fraternity, which might seem a little odd to an American. It's the French, we think, who have "Liberty, Equality, Fraternity." Not the Americans. And yet American nationalists too must distinguish between strangers and brothers, noncitizens and citizens. They must feel a special sense of fraternity with their fellow citizens. That's the logic of nationalism. Otherwise it's a hollow fraud.

The nationalist will prefer fellow citizens over noncitizens. He'll deny to noncitizens rights and privileges he grants to fellow citizens. But what he denies the noncitizen must then be paid for by what he would give to his fellow citizens. If the nationalist wants to reduce immigration, for example, he must argue that this will benefit citizens. By contrast, the antinationalist can treat citizens and noncitizens alike. If he is a progressive, he might want to offer the same generous welfare rights to each. If he is a libertarian, he might prefer to deny welfare rights to both groups. Nationalism, on the other hand, is about differences, about preferences for fellow citizens. Along with his love of liberty and equality, the American nationalist must prize fraternity.

Fraternity is the cement of society. More than a common belief in some grand theory of politics, it's the sense of fraternity that lets us accept the result of an election that our side lost fairly—rather than join in a "resistance" or talk about secession. It is what permits us to accept economic inequalities that are justly derived, and to oppose those that stem from unjust advantages.

Trump understood this. Read his speeches and you'll see how he reaches out to all Americans. And his sense of fraternity—his nationalism—went hand in hand with his belief in a strong safety net for American citizens. He wouldn't just repeal Obamacare, he would replace it with something better. And it was his sense of fraternity that most incensed his opponents. For the liberals, it was his solidarity with people they thought deplorable. For the libertarians who really didn't care much one way or the other about either citizens or noncitizens, it was the safety net he'd offer Americans. For both he was toxic, for all the wrong reasons.

Nationalism is more than a duty to look after fellow citizens. It's also one of the particularistic emotions that bind us to others, like love of family and friends, creating the sense of solidarity or community that is one of the most basic of human goods. Simone Weil called this "the need for roots,"[11] and it's especially needed in today's America. Between 1985 and 2004, the number of Americans who reported that they had told a friend something of personal importance to themselves during the prior six months fell from 73 to 51 percent, while the number of people who said they had no confidant with whom they discussed personal matters rose from 10 to 25 percent.[12] That is a staggering loss in social solidarity. In our loneliness, in the animosities that divide us, there has never been a greater need for fraternity.

A sense of nationalism doesn't exclude an affinity with or reliance upon more encompassing groups and institutions, such as the Western civilization that Trump praised in his Warsaw speech, or the United Nations to which he pledged his support in his September 2017 speech to the General Assembly. But in that speech Trump defended the idea of nationalism, for his and for all countries. "Our success depends on a coalition of strong and independent nations that embrace their sovereignty, to promote security, prosperity, and peace, for themselves and for the world." What nationalism meant to Trump was not zero-sum rivalries, but mutually beneficial cooperation among different nations. "Strong sovereign nations let diverse countries with different values, different cultures, and different dreams not just coexist, but work side by side on the basis of mutual respect." Trump is not a globalist who denies the value in nationalism, but an internationalist whose vision of global harmony is rooted in independent nations, each pursuing its own interests.

The nationalist will also recognize that nationalism can be taken too far, as when Europe blundered into the First World War, or when rogue nations such as North Korea pursue a madly aggressive foreign policy. In situations of this kind, even a nationalist might enlist the aid of a transnational body, or appeal to some ground of transnational solidarity. In the 1914 Christmas Truce, portrayed in the film *Joyeux Noël*, this was Christendom. Today, transnational solidarity might take the form of the UN Security Council, to which the Trump administration submitted a resolution to impose new sanctions against North Korea.

Our common humanity means something too, and the Christian cannot be indifferent to the suffering of people in other countries. We might thus support a welcoming refugee policy, generous foreign aid packages for starving countries, rescue efforts after national emergencies abroad. What is not required is indifference between the welfare of Americans and non-Americans. It's only when governments don't seem to care about their own that people turn inward and stop caring about people in other countries.

National governments can demand too much and turn oppressive. So too can families. But that's not an argument against the affection one naturally feels for one's nation or one's family. There are things we do not understand, observed Matthew Arnold, unless we understand that they are beautiful. So too, there are things we do not understand unless we understand that they are loved.

CHAPTER 9

HOW TO BRING BACK OUR MOJO

In Chapter 6, we saw how Canada is much more mobile than we are. If the country we so closely resemble got things right, we're bound to ask why it's beating the pants off us in terms of mobility. To answer this question, we need to rule out what's similar between the two countries and look for the differences that matter. At the same time, we need to identify the advantages enjoyed by the richest Americans and the barriers to advancement for the rest, and see how the playing field is leveled in Canada.

It isn't hard to find the differences in political and economic policies that explain why Canada is so mobile. Canada offers more choice for parents in K–12 education, and its high school students are much better educated than ours. Second, it's got a vastly superior immigration system, and Canadian immigrants are much less of a drag on mobility levels than are immigrants to America. Third, Canada is less heavily regulated than the United States. These are the policies that have made the difference, and in each case Trump proposes to mimic Canada.

TWO-TIER SCHOOLS

Among the reasons we're less mobile than Canada, the most important is probably our educational system. This is where the wealthiest Americans have a big advantage over other Americans, the ability to send their children to superior schools. At the top end, the rich can afford to place their children in superb private schools such as Sidwell Friends in Washington, D.C., the $40,000-a-year school to which the Clintons and the Obamas sent their children. And who could blame them, as parents? Everyone knows that D.C.'s public schools are substandard.

For the top 10 percent, schools in the suburbs also work. Access to good public schools is largely a matter of one's Zip Code, and ringing the District are the five richest counties in America. Their steep home prices reflect the quality of their local schools, and serve to exclude poorer Americans. For those who can afford to live there, this is a form of school choice.

In Canada, school choice wasn't just for the elites. Had I remained in Montreal, I could have sent my daughter to an English Catholic school, an English Protestant school, a French Catholic school, a French Protestant school or a Jewish school, all state-supported. The denominational and even linguistic differences mattered less to parents than the quality of the school. It's not just in Canada, either. Paradoxically, countries with established or quasi-established churches are comfortable with granting state funding to religious schools of various denominations and faiths, and people in those countries might therefore be thought to enjoy greater religious freedom than we do. Britain and Canada found it easy to subsidize both Catholic and Protestant schools, while in America this is regarded as an impermissible establishment of religion.

When schools have to compete for students, they offer a better service. You can see how competition works when you buy toothpaste at the drug store, and it also works when you choose a school for your children. State monopolies aren't very good when it comes to making cars, and they aren't much good when it comes to K–12 education. The difference between a competitive system and a monopolistic one is huge. Economists report that going from a system without any private schools to a system where half the schools are private increases the achievement level by substantially more than one year's learning in mathematics.[1] It's better still when private schools receive public financing or parents get vouchers they can take to any school they choose. That gives middle-class and poor parents a greater choice of schools, and even the children who remain in public school will benefit from the competition.

This explains why Canadian K–12 schools are so much better than ours. On the OECD's Program for International Student Assessment (PISA) tests of fifteen-year-olds (as shown in Appendix 4), we're a complete embarrassment in comparison with Canada. The academic achievement gap has enormous economic consequences. One study concluded that if the performance of American public school students were raised to Canadian levels, the gain to the U.S. economy would amount to a 20 percent annual pay increase for the average American worker.[2]

School choice is mostly what's different about the Western countries that beat us on educational tests. It's not as if we're spending too little on education. American K–12 teachers are among the best paid in the world, but that doesn't translate into student achievement. There are sizable differences in per-pupil expenditures among the states, but those spending levels don't correlate with test scores. And when we compare ourselves with other countries, there's no correlation between dollars spent and PISA scores.[3]

The feeble American response to school choice has been charter schools, made weaker still by the efforts of public sector unions to ensure that they'll be blocked, or underfunded, or micromanaged if they're tolerated. American charters are too often poorly organized, ground-up schools that lack the institutional resources and reputational advantages of an established sectarian school. The Jesuits have been in the education business for five hundred years. No charter school could ever compete with that.

When liberals interview me about how our schools rank alongside those of Canada and other countries, I can expect a few smirks. *You're trying to tell me we should care what happens elsewhere? We don't. We are Klingons!* And then they'll allude to what they delicately call "demographic differences." What they mean by this (though they'll never actually say it) is that the United States has a large minority population, while the Great White North is basically an English- and French-speaking Iceland. Take our minorities out of the mix, and we'd do just as well, they think. Except none of this is true. Canada is 20 percent foreign-born (versus 13 percent in the U.S.), and has a sizable minority population. And when you compare only America's white kids with *all* of Canada's kids, the Canadians still do considerably better.[4] Of course the liberal's implicit racism is nasty. It's also shameful to suggest that a third of our children are less than American and that it's permitted to warehouse them in third-rate schools.

The purveyors of elite, liberal opinion—NPR, the *Atlantic*,[5] the *New Yorker*[6]—tell us that we need to send kids to public schools in order to

socialize them in American values. Those "American values" aren't especially American, however. Increasingly, our public schools ignore great
American heroes in favor of all the things that are wrong with America.
For religious parents, public education can seem more like an indoctrination in progressive notions than real education. Our public schools
do an abysmal job of teaching English, math and science, but make up
for it with lectures on gender fluidity, beginning in kindergarten.[7] As
the *Washington Post* admiringly notes, "some city and suburban school
boards are shedding their stodgy reputation and staking out ardent
positions on political and social issues. Skeptics question the utility or
appropriateness of those declarations, but some boards view decrying
gender and racial inequity as part of their professional duty."[8]

Given the political indoctrination and the abysmal quality of our
public schools, what justification can there be for opposing school
choice? There are no constitutional obstacles to voucher plans at the
federal level. The Supreme Court has blessed public vouchers that can
be used at religiously affiliated schools, provided that parents have the
option of sending their kids to local public schools.[9] Yet thirty-eight
states erected constitutional barriers to public funds going to parochial
schools, through the nineteenth-century "Blaine Amendments," which
were motivated by the anti-Catholic bigotry of the time.[10] While the
anti-Catholicism faded, the legal barriers remained in place, sustained by
self-interested teacher unions and the discreet bigotry of a secular elite.[11]

Those teacher unions and their PTA allies have tremendous political clout in the U.S., and they don't like competition. The National
Education Association and the American Federation of Teachers together
have a membership of 4.5 million, or 2.9 percent of the American workforce. In Canada, K–12 teachers and school employees make up only 1.4
percent of the workforce. Somehow Canada beats the U.S. hands down
in K–12 education with less than half the teaching staff. That should be
embarrassing.

There's also the preference of upper-class parents for an aristocracy.[12]
Fixing public schools wouldn't mean that upper-class children get a poor
education, but it does mean they would face more competition from
below when they go on to college and careers. That accounts for the
New Class's seemingly pathological desire to ensure that other people's
children enjoy the dubious blessings of a public school education. If their

own children are to succeed, it is necessary that other people's children fail. That might seem odd. Even the bird of prey knows not to foul its own nest. But then for the New Class it's not their own nest. It's the nest of the Other. The deplorables.

Happily, Trump has called school choice the great civil rights issue of our time. Then, at the 2017 Values Voter Summit, he told religious conservatives, "my plan will break the government monopoly and make schools compete to provide the best services for our children. The money will follow the student to the public, private or religious school that is best for them and their family." The budget he handed Congress called for $1.4 billion to be allocated to voucher programs that parents could use to pay for tuition at private or religious schools, and he suggested that in time this might be ramped up to a $20 billion program.[13] Were this to happen, it would amount to one of the most remarkable reforms we could see from a Trump administration, and would help bring our dismal K–12 system up to Canadian and world standards. And it would greatly help restore the American Dream, the idea that this is a country where our children will have it better than we did.

MAIDS AND GARDENERS FOR THE NEW CLASS

I became an American on April 15, 2014. That's right, Tax Day. "Welcome to America," they told me. "Here's the bill." Since then I've taken a keen interest in immigration, and I've learned to separate the big from the small issues.

Donald Trump's ninety-day ban on immigrants from six majority-Muslim nations was a small issue. The executive order affected a few thousand refugees, as compared with the million immigrants naturalized each year under the Immigration and Nationality Act of 1965. And that act is a mess. It admits people who underbid native-born Americans for low-skill jobs, while refusing entry to people with greater skills who would make life better for Americans. To top it off, we admit fifty thousand people a year just because they won a lottery. That's how we got Sayfullo Habibullaevic Saipov, the terrorist who plowed a truck into pedestrians and cyclists in New York City in October 2017. It doesn't get crazier than that. We're the world's preferred destination for emigrants, and it's a scandal that we're not more selective about who gets in.

To be clear, the problem isn't that our present immigration policies make the country poorer. When economists run the numbers, those policies don't appear to be costly on net. The most widely respected immigration scholar, George Borjas, concludes that one really can't say.[14] The new arrivals benefit native consumers by producing goods and services more cheaply, but at the same time, the cheaper maid or gardener might be taking a job away from the native-born. Add it all up and it seems like a wash.

That's not the end of it, however, for three reasons. First, our immigration policies make America more immobile. We accept immigrants who will earn less than the average native-born American, and the difference persists over two generations. U.S. immigrants earn 20 percent less than native-born Americans, their children will earn 10 percent less and their grandchildren 5 percent less.[15]

Second, even if immigration on net is an economic zero, it still creates winners and losers, and results in a wealth transfer from poor to rich Americans. The wealthy are better off when their goods and services are produced more cheaply by immigrants, but these gains come at a cost to poorer Americans who lose their jobs or whose wages are pushed down by competition with immigrant labor. Borjas reports that increasing the immigrant flow by 10 percent depressed the earnings of native-born Americans by 4 percent between 1960 and 2010.[16] These costs are felt most by black Americans, and a 10 percent increase in immigration was associated with a 5.9 percent reduction in the black employment rate.[17]

The third problem with our immigration policies is the opportunity cost of failing to seek higher-quality immigrants. Even if immigrants had the same skill sets as the native-born, that's not the highest of bars, as we saw in the previous section. Why not bring in the best? And that's what the immigration reform bill introduced by Senators Tom Cotton (R-AR) and Dale Perdue (R-GA), and backed by Trump, would do. The bill, called the RAISE Act, would copy the Canadian points system, which is generally considered the model for immigration reform.[18]

The points system has given Canada immigrants who are more skilled than their American counterparts, and who assimilate more quickly into the national economy.[19] It has also given Canada smart teenagers who boost the country's PISA scores (as we saw in the last chapter), and the BBC tells us this is why Canada has become an "education superpower."[20] It's also been argued that if we mimicked Canada and required better skills or job credentials from immigrants, we might significantly lower the tax burden for the native-born.[21] Finally, if we wanted to make America more mobile, immigration reform along Canadian lines would be a good place to begin. Unlike second-generation Americans, second-generation Canadians are as well educated and as likely to be employed as the children of native-born Canadians.[22]

Right now, a country little more than a tenth the size of the U.S. in population actually admits about as many economic migrants a year as we do, with the goal of making the native-born better off financially. And while money isn't everything, economic criteria are a pretty good proxy for the private virtues we'd like to see in immigrants. That explains why Canada can admit so many immigrants each year without it becoming a political issue. It also explains why the country has a generous refugee program. Canadians see an immigration policy designed to benefit the native-born, so they don't think their government wants to stick it to them with its refugee policy.

It's a different story here. Our current immigration system has protected the New Class from competition with high-skilled immigrants, while at the same time giving the richest Americans cheap maids and gardeners. It's hard to see much social justice in any of this. It's also hard to see much reason to resist the merit-based Canadian system. While some critics may think a merit-based system is camouflage for racism (a charge that betrays racist assumptions itself), the Canadian system is anything but racist. Between 2006 and 2011, about 160,000 European-born immigrants arrived in Canada, amounting to 14 percent of the total, but more than 660,000, or 55 percent of all immigrants, came from Asia or the Middle East.[23] The big difference between the current immigration policies of the U.S. and Canada is that Canada prefers high-skilled immigrants while the U.S. favors low-skilled immigrants. Canada will admit highly skilled Nigerians while excluding low-skilled ones. Hard to see much racism there.

Another problem with our current immigration system is, of course, the eleven million undocumented "illegals" in America, predominantly from Mexico. While Trump said "they're not sending us their best people," the fact is that most illegals are here to work, not to deal drugs. They're the people who hang around the lumberyards looking for day labor, and they're the maids who clean the houses of America's New Class. They're less likely than legal immigrants to abuse our welfare system, since applying for government benefits raises the risk of discovery and deportation. Nevertheless, they're taking jobs from Americans. Of those eleven million illegals, about eight million are in the workforce, and of these nearly two-thirds (five million people) crossed the border from Mexico. Were they not here, some of the jobs they take would simply disappear. Some lawyers would mow their own lawns and mop their own floors, and the Zoë Bairds and Kimba Woods might have had to raise their kids themselves instead of dumping them on illegal nannies.[24] But some of those jobs would still exist and would be done by Americans at higher pay if we had an effective southern border wall.

That's simply the economics of supply and demand. Restrict the supply of labor, and watch wages go up. That was clear in 2017, when California garlic farmers couldn't fill all their needs with illegal labor at $11 an hour and found they had to hire American citizens at $13 an hour. They're afraid they might have to offer $15 an hour this year.[25] That's the same wage that progressives mandated by law in Seattle, which has resulted in killing American jobs, yet they support an immigration amnesty that would have the result of denying real jobs at $15 an hour to American workers. Hypocrisy doesn't get much more rank than that.

THE NEW CLASS'S BRIAR PATCH

Until fairly recently, the rule of law wasn't on too many people's radar screen. When it comes to what makes a country rich, liberals talked about the importance of infrastructure (for example, a good highway system), while conservatives pushed for privatization as a more efficient way to provide goods and services. But none of that matters as much as a legal regime that protects property rights and enforces contracts, and that doesn't fetter us with excessive regulation. This constitutes what we call the rule of law, and according to the World Bank it accounts for 44 percent of a country's total wealth.[26]

America isn't the poster child for the rule of law. The World Justice Project (WJP) ranks countries on that basis, and reports that we come in at eighteenth among thirty-six First World nations (with Canada at eleventh). The problem isn't that we have too little law, like Afghanistan and other failed states. America's problem is just the opposite: too much law, an uncountable number of federal crimes, a vague set of private law rules, a humungous list of administrative rules. America gets high marks for the ease of starting a business, but thereafter the new firm must confront a vague and uncertain set of criminal and civil liability rules, as well as regulatory barriers that can turn honest businessmen into unwitting felons.

We confront the twin hurdles of opaqueness and extensiveness, of rules that are difficult to understand and that touch almost everything you do. It's what Ortega y Gasset called "plenitude," the profusion of rules that squeezes out what formerly was unencumbered activity, through the multiplication of veto players whose permission is required before things can be done. "What previously was, in general, no problem, now begins to be an everyday one, namely, to find room."[27]

Plenitude in this sense is a consequence of the accretion of rules over time, as Mancur Olson explained.[28] A government breeds interest groups that invest in both rules and rule makers, so that over time it becomes harder to pare back any of the rules and return to square one. The thing grows like Topsy, one rule added upon another, until a simple reform becomes a thousand-page bill and sprouts twenty thousand pages of regulations. The result is sclerosis, the inability to get anything done without hordes of lawyers at your side.

Why has it become so bad? One big reason is because the administrative state is the briar patch in which the New Class lives. The tangle of rules and regulations is a virtually impenetrable barrier for non-adepts, the small businessmen and workers who compose the bottom 90 percent of Americans. But the top 10 percent thrive in the thicket. The administrative state provides direct employment for many of them as civil servants, and indirect employment for the far greater number of lawyers, lobbyists and economists hired to navigate it and shape its rules. At a further remove, the major corporations, charities and institutions that occupy the economy's commanding heights employ the outside lawyers, the compliance experts, the human relations team and the government relations departments that find easy passageways around regulatory rules. If we've grown an aristocracy, the rise of the administrative state is surely one of the reasons. And if we're living in an overregulated administrative state, it's in no small measure because an aristocratic New Class writes the rules.

In his acceptance speech at the Republican National Convention, Trump said that regulatory overload is one of our biggest job killers: "Excessive regulation is costing our country as much as $2 trillion a year, and we will end it." His economic agenda spoke to the fears of Americans that we're falling behind, that our children will fare worse than we did, and he promised to do something about it. Regulatory reform must be part of the package.

If we want to make America mobile again, the way back is simple enough. Fix our broken schools. Amend our immigration laws. Return to the rule of law. And yet those who boast of their concern about immobility are the very members of the New Class who oppose all such reforms, who for self-interested reasons would keep things just as they are, unequal, immobile. Cruel hypocrites! You might plead your ignorance, but your self-deception only makes it worse.

CHAPTER 10

WHAT IS A JOBS PRESIDENT?

A fter he was elected president, George H. W. Bush announced that he intended to be an "education president." Harry Jaffa, a political philosopher at Claremont, mischievously asked, "is education an adjective?" Behind the snark was an astute question: Just what is an education president anyway? Was it something like the line that Bush mistakenly read out from an index card during one of his speeches, "Message: I care"?

Trump has said he wants to be known as the "jobs president," but just what does that mean? What does it take to get America working again, to give Americans a sense of earned self-worth? As it happens, Trump has the good fortune to follow Barack Obama, who provided an excellent example of what a jobs president should *not* do: enact job-killing laws, let regulators tie up the economy in knots, pursue the chimera of "green energy jobs" while hobbling job creators in the rest of the energy field. And we can see the result by looking at our labor force participation.

The labor force participation rate measures the number of people who are either working or actively seeking work, as a percentage of all over-sixteen Americans who aren't in prison or in active military service. That number increased as women entered the labor force in the latter part of the twentieth century, but in recent years it has markedly declined. From a rate of 67.3 percent in 2000, it's fallen to 63 percent. For prime-age men (25–54 years), Italy is the only OECD country with a lower labor force participation rate than the U.S.

According to the best liberal economists, Obama was doing

everything possible to boost employment. The administration and the Federal Reserve had tried every trick in the Keynesian playbook: flooding the market with money in order to get people spending, near-zero interest rates, cash for clunkers, home buyer tax credits, mortgage relief plans. We maxed out on the government's easy-money credit card, and all we got was the slowest recovery from any recession since the Second World War and a jobless recovery at that.

Obama's apologists have blamed the decline in the labor force participation rate on baby boomers who retired. It's true that the rate is affected by demographic trends over which governments have no control, but the decline also reflects the numbers of people who have become discouraged by the absence of jobs in a weak economy and have given up looking for work. If it were all a matter of demographics, we should be tied with Canada. Only we aren't. We trail Canada by 2.5 percentage points.[1] At Canada's rate, we would have an additional four million jobs, which is almost the size of the total labor force in Virginia. So one lesson for a jobs president is: emulate Canada.

TAX REFORM

The 2017 tax reform legislation—the Tax Cuts and Jobs Act—mimics Canada's tax policies and promises to bring jobs back to America. It reduces corporate taxes to 21 percent, down from 35 percent. The former rate was one of the highest in the world, and if you added in state taxes it was 39.1 percent on average, the highest rate in the G20.[2] By comparison, the Canadian federal rate is just 15 percent. There's a worldwide competition for investment dollars, and other things being equal they're going to flow to low-tax countries. Copy them, and the jobs will follow.

American firms have parked $2.5 trillion of earnings offshore because taxes are lower in other countries. That's one reason why multinationals shed 2.9 million U.S. jobs in the first decade of this century, while increasing overseas employment by 2.4 million.[3] With the new 21 percent corporate tax rate, the cross-country differences are now much smaller, and there's less reason to keep earnings abroad. In addition, under the new law, American firms with money parked abroad must pay a tax of between 8 and 15 percent on it. Thereafter they can repatriate the moneys back to the U.S. tax-free.

Until now we've been sending jobs offshore with our tax laws. The 2017 tax reform promises to make the United States a tax haven and jobs magnet.

SKILLS TRAINING

The tax reform bill will result in a higher demand for American workers, but the data show that to get people working we need to do more than increase demand. There's also the matter of supply, of the stock of well-trained workers who can fill the jobs. After all, we've seen plenty of job openings go unfilled. The Bureau of Labor Statistics reports that there are 5.7 million job openings in the U.S. Those jobs would employ 3.7 percent of the labor force, which is not much less than the unemployment rate of 4.1 percent. If everyone looking for work took one of the unfilled jobs, the unemployment rate would be less than half a percent. So how come the jobs aren't being taken up? There are three reasons.

The first reason is occupational snobbism. It's all very well to say that there's a job opening in garbage disposal, but that's not going to appeal to an out-of-work tax preparer. Snobbism is too harsh a term for the tax preparer who lacks the strength to hoist a trash can, of course. But still, there are a good many jobs that go unfilled because of social stigma and stereotypes. Mike Rowe, former star of Discovery Channel's *Dirty Jobs* and CNN's *Somebody's Gotta Do It*, was perplexed to find that small-business owners hung out "Help Wanted" signs but couldn't hire people in the depths of the recent Great Recession. There's not much we can do about that, except tweak the rules for unemployment benefits to make any job look better than none, or wait for employers to offer higher wages.

The second reason why jobs go unfilled is geography. A job opening in Seattle might not appeal to an unemployed West Virginia coal miner. That's an explanation that Tyler Cowen of George Mason University trots out in *The Complacent Class*.[4] We're less likely today to pick up stakes and move to another town or another state in search of a better job, and it's because we've become lazy and unwilling to get off our duffs, says Cowen. For the New Class, that's a comforting thought, but the empirical evidence about laziness isn't there. What's different today is the disappearance of jobs in a declining economy.[5]

The third reason for unfilled jobs is a mismatch between the skills of job seekers and the requirements of available jobs. This is the explanation that Claudia Goldin and Lawrence F. Katz give for the decline in labor force participation rates.[6] More people are going on to college than in the past, but they're being educated for jobs that aren't there: literary deconstructionist, feminist, social justice warrior. It's a supply-side problem. There are jobs waiting to be filled, but we aren't producing workers with the skill sets needed to fill them.

Too often, students are taking courses that mark them as disasters waiting to happen. Would you want to hire someone whose college transcript includes courses like Oberlin's "Beginning Dungeons and Dragons," Cornell's tree-climbing course or USC's course on selfies? Apart from the ridiculous courses, the student mobs that have shut down visiting campus speakers at places like Middlebury and UC Berkeley have done nothing to make college students look like attractive hires.

To remedy this, Trump has proposed better skills training, with an emphasis on the jobs that are out there. This would include online learning and public-private apprenticeship programs, courses "that prepare people for trade, manufacturing, technology, and other really well-paying jobs and careers."[7] What he has in mind is vocational training, not a four-year B.A., and this has bothered critics who think that it slights the broad, humanistic learning that American universities are imagined to provide.[8] But humanistic learning doesn't describe what's happening today in most of our universities, even the best of them. Rather, what students are getting is simply another kind of vocational training, where the vocation is membership in the New Class of lawyers, government aides and NGO staffers. It's not humanistic education so much as coaching in how our clever barbarians might master cultural signifiers in order to join a credentialed elite.

DISABILITY AND WELFARE REFORM

More Americans would be at work today if not for our inflated disability rates. Alan Krueger reports that a third of prime-age men not in the labor force say they're disabled, compared with 2.6 percent of prime-age employed men.[9] Those not in the labor force report the highest levels of pain, and they're more likely to use pain-killing opioids. The National Institute on Drug Abuse tells us that two million Americans have a substance use disorder, and that between 8 and 12 percent of those who were prescribed an opioid subsequently became hooked.[10]

Our welfare policies plausibly give people an incentive to claim that they're disabled and to drop out of the labor force. They're then apt to be prescribed pain-killing drugs such as OxyContin. Along with related federal and state programs, Social Security Disability Insurance (SSDI) offers a generous welfare check for people whose pain and disability prevent them from working. There are now eleven million Americans on SSDI, or 6.8 percent of the total labor force, up from 2.2 percent in 1985. Another eight million claimants receive aid from the Supplemental Social Insurance (SSI) program, and a further 3.5 million under the VA disability program. It's unlikely that the number of people with a debilitating condition could really have increased that much in a generation or so. What changed was 1984 legislation that placed more weight on applicants' *self-reported* pain and discomfort as the basis for receiving SSDI. The benefits also increased, from 68 to 86 percent of one's salary.[11]

Our welfare programs were well intended but can have perverse incentives. I saw the same phenomenon at work with Ron Hunt, one of my favorite baseball players. Hunt was a journeyman second baseman for the old Montreal Expos, but had one singular talent: hogging the plate when he was at bat. When the Expos had the bases loaded and Hunt was up, he'd lean in and get hit by a pitch. He was then awarded first base and would walk home a run. For a .220 hitter, it beat trying to get on base the usual way. Hunt simply took advantage of what the system offered, demonstrating that when you subsidize something, you'll get more of it—even pain.

And that's seemingly what happened to our jobs numbers. When we paid more to people who said they were in pain, more people reported that they were in pain, stopped working and took painkillers. It was Ron Hunt all over again.[12]

So we need to tailor our welfare programs to reduce the incentive to claim a disability without need. The Trump budget proposes to test new approaches to increase labor force participation, including getting SSDI and SSI recipients back to work if they are able. It would cut $72.5

billion over ten years from programs for the disabled, including SSDI and SSI. Trump also proposes to get welfare recipients back to work by rolling back Obama-era waivers from the workfare requirements of the 1996 welfare reform act. Trump's critics have called all this ruthless, but any discussion of the government's policies for the disabled and welfare recipients should begin with an understanding of their perverse incentives.

FOREIGN POLICY AND INFRASTRUCTURE SPENDING

During the George W. Bush administration, Democrats complained that the Iraq war was draining our resources and that the money would be better spent on infrastructure. The war was killing Americans. Infrastructure spending would give them jobs. It was a good argument, and it helped elect a Democratic Congress in 2006.

That wasn't how Bush had seen it. In 2002, I attended a small meeting at the White House, where Bush briefed us on his war aims just moments before he signed the Authorization for Use of Military Force Against Iraq. So if anyone knows why we went to war, it's me. Someone asked Bush, "Won't this be expensive?" Bush smiled. "That's the beauty of it. It won't cost a thing. They have all that oil." We were just going to take it for ourselves. He really believed that. But it didn't turn out that way, and in his campaign Trump went out of his way to criticize Bush and his neoconservative supporters for the Iraq debacle.

Trump complained that the war was wasteful, that it was poorly conducted, that our allies weren't paying their fair share. He connected excessive spending on foreign wars with the money we could otherwise have spent at home on infrastructure and jobs. That's what the Democrats had said, but Trump added an element of class conflict by siding with an underclass that bore the brunt of our military adventures.

TRADE BARRIERS?

In his campaign speeches, Trump complained that other countries were robbing us blind in our trade deals. We're shipping jobs offshore, he said, and with better trade agreements we could bring jobs back to America. That might be true, but figuring it out requires an understanding of arcane trade details that I have no desire to master. I've given myself a pass on the vexed question of Canadian softwood lumber.

I've also learned to mistrust the ideologues on both sides of the free-trade debate. The pure free trader is certainly correct in thinking that trade barriers reduce worldwide wealth. He might even be right to believe that a country could increase its GDP by unilaterally eliminating all trade barriers. But I think he's wrong to think that wealth transfer effects within a country should be ignored. A move to free trade will benefit some Americans—the consumers who can buy cheaper foreign-made goods—at a cost to other Americans—the workers who see their jobs shipped overseas. Perhaps you don't care about this if you're a libertarian. But then you might also want to dismantle the entire welfare state.

If the free trader can seem heartless, the trade protectionist can come across as naive. At a White House briefing, I heard Trump spend five minutes talking about China and twenty minutes denouncing our trade deal with Canada under NAFTA. It sounded like a *South Park* "Blame Canada" video, but without the punch lines. While there are always small differences to be resolved, trade agreements are a matter of give-ups and gets, of things traded away for things more valuable, and that certainly was true when Canada-U.S. free trade was negotiated thirty years ago. Today, this is the world's largest bilateral trade relationship and a model for other countries. In particular, the two economies are so closely integrated, with just-in-time production, that closing the border would instantly mean the loss of many thousands of American jobs, especially in the auto sector. More trade passes over a single bridge between Michigan and Ontario than our entire trade with Japan, and it's been estimated that eight million U.S. jobs depend on exports to Canada. Doubtless, the agreement needs to be updated, and aggressive posturing can be a useful negotiating tool, but it was chilling to hear a White House aide boasting to me afterward that "we came *this close* to withdrawing from NAFTA."

The protectionist is also naive about how trade policies get decided in America. He's correct to think that we should take the interests of American workers into account, but he's wrong to believe that wishing will make it so. Trade barriers will be set in Washington, where the thumbs of donors and lobbyists weigh heavily on the scale, and they won't be representing America's underclass. The trade barriers that benefit America's sugar producers while raising sugar prices 64 to 92 percent above the world average are a good example.[13] They don't do anything for jobs, and the burden lies heaviest upon poorer Americans, who spend a higher proportion of their earnings on food. And yet the Trump administration wants to renew the tariff.

That's why I suspend judgment about whether renegotiating our trade deals will help American workers. As between the ideologues for and against free trade, I don't have to take sides.

CHAPTER 11

DRAINING THE SWAMP

On the campaign trail, Donald Trump promised to drain the "swamp." Everyone seemed to know what that meant, even if they would have been hard pressed to define it. They simply felt that something was rotten in the state of Denmark. Since the election, however, the swamp has come to be identified with the "deep state," an unelected fourth branch of government formed by the many thousands of civilian federal workers who create, interpret and administer the rules we live by. Because they are virtually impossible to dislodge, they make ordinary Americans feel helpless, like peasants in an absolute monarchy. And the deep state bites back. Senator Chuck Schumer (D-NY) warned Trump not to criticize the intelligence community. "Let me tell you, . . . they have six ways from Sunday at getting back at you."[1]

There was a time when rogue CIA employees who ignored our elected leaders were considered a threat to democracy. In 1975, a Senate committee chaired by Frank Church (D-ID) revealed that the agency had spied on Americans and attempted to kill foreign leaders. Later that year, in *Three Days of the Condor*, Robert Redford portrayed a heroic CIA analyst whom the agency tries to kill because he's discovered their plans to seize Middle East oil fields. But when the president is Trump, the tables are turned and the deep state suddenly becomes the good guys. When Mike Pompeo was appointed Trump's CIA director in January 2017, he at first did the agency's bidding. But when Pompeo began to push back, the *Washington Post* reported that he'd become a source of "apprehension" in the agency's upper ranks.[2] It's what Chuck Schumer warned Trump to expect.

Michael J. Glennon has described how a foreign policy establishment constrains the options open to a newly elected president.[3] He'll appoint the secretary of state, the secretary of defense, the CIA director, the national security advisor, and they'll choose people a level or two down, but beneath them is a national security bureaucracy, many of whom are carryovers from a previous administration. They'll inform the higher-ups which policy and personnel choices are open to them, and which are not. Behind them are the old foreign policy mandarins, people whose claims of special expertise are often taken at face value, even though they were responsible for twenty years of foreign policy failures. Before the election, the mandarins on the right even thought themselves able to hobble a Trump administration by announcing that they wouldn't work for him. That was supposed to be a threat.

BACK TO JUSTINIAN

The deep foreign policy state is simply one part of the swamp, and not the costliest one either. It hadn't been on Trump's radar screen during the campaign. Instead he spoke about the economic costs imposed by agencies such as the Environmental Protection Agency and the Consumer Financial Protection Bureau. With them in mind, he said in a New Hampshire town hall that "70 percent of regulations can go."

A lot of people agree with him. It's generally believed that the regulatory state has developed a severe case of elephantiasis, and that this is a leading cause of the decline in American economic growth. The Code of Federal Regulations was 175,000 pages long in 2013, and the Federal Register, which contains new rules, proposed rules and public notices, is 70,000 pages long *each year*. Before a new rule goes into effect, the Administrative Procedure Act requires agencies to issue a notice and allow a period for public comment. That was supposed to slow things down. Evidently it didn't. In addition, agencies often circumvent the notice-and-comment requirement by hiding their rules in detailed handbooks and staff manuals, not to mention the advice they might offer over the phone or in letters to affected parties.

To give but one example, the Obama administration's Deferred Action on Parents of Americans (DAPA) granted five million illegal aliens immunity from deportation and gave them work permits. It read like a statute, but it wasn't one, and it wasn't even a regulation or executive order. Instead, it was a memorandum from the Homeland Security secretary. The federal Fifth Circuit Court deemed it an improper attempt to sidestep administrative review, and on appeal the Supreme Court split 4-4.[4] That was just one among countless bureaucratic memoranda and regulations, virtually none of which will ever end up before the courts.

The 70 percent cut to the CFR that Trump proposed would bring us down to the more manageable page counts of 1972, and this can have a beneficial result. One study concluded that if regulations had been held constant at 1980 levels, the U.S. economy would have been about 25 percent larger in 2012, and each American would have been $13,000 richer.[5] How to get back to 1980 regulatory levels is the hard part.

Economically significant rules (with a price tag north of $100 million a year) require a cost-benefit analysis from the federal government's Office of Information and Regulatory Affairs. But that analysis turns out to be highly politicized, and in Democratic administrations the benefit always seems to exceed the cost. This tends to produce a one-way ratchet in which regulations expand in Democratic administrations and then prove impossible to reverse in Republican ones. Trump issued an executive order directing federal agencies to find two rules to eliminate for every new rule proposed, but that can be done only by going through the notice-and-comment provisions of the Administrative Procedure Act. Each rollback has to be separately justified, and that takes time. The APA was supposed to protect us from a regulatory nightmare, but it's had the opposite effect, preventing us from eliminating excess regulations. What it protects is the continued dominance of the deep state.

We've seen it before. In 527 A.D., the Byzantine emperor Justinian looked at the state of Roman law, contained in about two thousand separate volumes written over hundreds of years, and decided that something had to be done with the superfluous rules. He appointed what today we'd call a law reform commission to restate all the laws. Rather than tinker with things, Justinian's commission discarded rules that were inefficient, obsolete, repetitive and confusingly overlapping, and produced the much shorter *Digest*. Laws not selected for the *Digest* were declared invalid and were not thereafter to be cited in the courts.

The Byzantine Empire fell in 1453, when Constantinople became Istanbul (and a hit novelty song for the Four Lads exactly five hundred years later). Justinian's Hagia Sophia, the Church of Holy Wisdom, was turned into a mosque and is now a museum. But the legal code he instituted, the *Corpus Iuris Civilis*, became the foundational document of the civil law of France and many other countries. "The vain titles of the victories of Justinian are crumbled into dust," wrote Edward Gibbon, "but the name of the legislator is inscribed on a fair and everlasting monument."[6]

Today we need another Justinian and another code that sweeps away a welter of rules so extensive and mind-numbingly detailed that no one can keep up with them. A modern regulatory-reform commission should be put to work, one composed of common-sense experts who are aware of both the good and bad things that regulations can do, and who are especially alert to the cost of the sheer number of rules, each of which might seem sensible by itself alone. The digest they propose should, on adoption by Congress, replace all existing rules and be exempted from APA review.

Could the commission really cut back regulations by 70 percent, as Trump proposed? Yes, and more, if it corrects three biases of the deep state's rule making. First, the commission should abandon the regulator's conceit that every little error deserves to be corrected by a rule. With that mistaken belief in mind, some regulator must have stumbled over a case where a consumer was confused at a grocery store, and made it a crime to sell "Turkey Ham" with the words "Turkey" and "Ham" in different fonts.

Second, the commission must recognize that we can't anticipate all future risks and eliminate them with a rule. The regulator's hubris that he could do so is what added twenty thousand pages of requirements to the thousand-page Dodd-Frank financial reform bill, without really lessening the risk of a financial meltdown.

Third, the commission should substitute general common-sense standards for detailed rules wherever possible. That's what another legal reformer, Napoleon, did in 1804 when his experts produced the French Civil Code, the basis for the private law of France, Italy, Spain, Belgium and the countries of Latin America. Napoleon's commission took the customary laws of the *ancien régime*, its statutes and decrees, and the wealth of laws from revolutionary France, and boiled them down to a much-shortened statement of legal principles. For example, all of the law of civil wrongs (torts) was reduced to two articles: "Any act of man, which causes damages to another, shall oblige the person by whose fault it occurred to repair it" (art. 1382); and, "One shall be liable not only by reason of one's acts, but also by reason of one's imprudence or negligence" (art. 1383).

When you think about it, not much more than that is needed. And more can, in fact, be harmful. Narrow regulations, such as "the board shall be one inch thick," betray the rule maker's hubris in assuming he can anticipate technological changes. What if new technology could make a half-inch board just as safe? The manufacturer would nevertheless be compelled to produce a wastefully thick board. Worse still, what if the one-inch board turned out to be unsafe after all? The manufacturer might be sued, but he'll plead, "I was only following the rules." That's why general standards ("the board shall be safe for consumers, taking costs into account") are superior to narrow rules, even apart from the way in which excessive rules become impossible to understand. And if an industry seeks the safe harbor of narrow rules, let these be produced by the industry itself, in the form of industry handbooks, periodically updated, rather than fossilized like a fly in regulatory amber.

With that in mind, it wouldn't be hard to staff a regulatory reform committee with able experts who could take an axe to the Code of Federal Regulations.

BACK TO ANDREW JACKSON

I watched the Trump inauguration from the polite and very civilized confines of the Canadian embassy on Pennsylvania Avenue. Elsewhere the city was in shock. But it was nothing compared with how official Washington had reacted to Andrew Jackson's inauguration in 1829. From the far-off West, in Kentucky and Ohio, Jackson's supporters poured into the federal city, jostling the locals and wandering about in gape-mouthed wonder. Some Washingtonians were reminded of the pillaging British troops that had arrived fifteen years earlier. When the oath of office was administered and everyone repaired to a White House reception, the scene was pure bedlam. Over tubs of punch, the frontiersman bumped into the congressman, whose wife was elbowed aside by the bargeman. Pickpockets had a field day. To Justice Joseph Story, the reign of "King Mob" seemed triumphant.[7]

The Mob was there to see their hero, of course, and to have a good time. But they were also there to find jobs in the new administration. There was no job tenure for civil servants in those days, and Jackson fired 10 percent of the federal workforce and replaced them with people loyal to him. That was the beginning of what came to be called the "spoils system," based on the principle that a president was entitled to replace the prior administration's civil servants with his own men. It's how Tammany Hall was able to fill up police and fire departments with loyal Democrats, and it's how Abraham Lincoln spent much of early 1861, worrying about who the postmasters were to be.

The spoils system was reversed with civil service reform, beginning with the 1883 Pendleton Act. That act did two things. It banned the pay-for-play practice of politicians who solicited campaign funds from job seekers. It also required certain appointments to be based on merit, through competitive exams. That eliminated a source of political corruption, and some thought the act had the further benefit of restricting the civil service to a better class of Americans and excluding the Jacksonian and Tammany Hall underclass.[8]

The reformers weren't troubled by their class biases, of course, and they subscribed to a vision of publicly interested bureaucrats who would mirror the views of their political masters. They would be Max Weber's selfless public servants, who would offer "the optimum possibility for carrying through the principle of specializing administrative functions according to purely objective considerations."[9] What could go wrong? With the arrival of public choice scholarship, however, the public interest model began to be doubted. In an influential book, Bill Niskanen modeled bureaucrats as self-interested actors who seek to maximize the size of their agency's budget.[10] Apart from their salaries and job security, bureaucrats also compensate themselves through the exercise of power, shaping the rules in ways they and not the elected officials want.

The bureaucrats even boast about it. After Trump's inauguration, the *Washington Post* reported that federal workers were "in regular consultation with recently departed Obama-era political appointees about what they can do to push back against the new president's initiatives."[11]

That might be a problem for any administration, but it's especially so for Trump, given the liberal political sympathies of federal workers.[12]

It's like having a servant who pilfers from you. You don't like it, but you don't want to do the household chores yourself either. And who can you call in to monitor the servant? That's where conservatives come up short in their proposals to bring the bureaucrats to heel. First, they'd like courts to second-guess the agencies and strike down more of their regulations. But lawyers and judges aren't trained in the scientific skills that regulators are called on to exercise. What courts offer is technical, procedural review, and not the substantive scrutiny that might tell us whether the rule is well designed and efficient. There's an administrative state in every First World country, and courts in each of them necessarily defer to the regulators. More importantly, courts are limited by their dockets and can't micromanage the many thousands of administrative rules, not without becoming part of the deep state themselves.

Second, conservatives want Congress to step in and review the agencies more closely. But it's Congress that created the problem by permitting the agencies to go their merry way, and it has little of the expertise needed to micromanage the regulators. More can be done, along the lines of the proposed REINS Act, which would require congressional approval for new rules that would impose compliance costs of more than $100 million a year. But since congressional staffers don't have much technical expertise, you'd probably see them approve virtually all the proposed big-ticket regulations. Nor would the REINS Act roll back any existing regulations.

It sounds like a new problem. It's not. It's something that Lord Hewart identified as far back as 1929. Recognizing how the administrative state had developed and stripped power from Britain's elected representatives in Parliament, he called it the "new despotism."[13] It became the subject of satire in the BBC comedy *Yes, Minister*, where a senior bureaucrat runs rings around a slightly befuddled cabinet minister. Lord Hewart's charge that the administrative state imperils democratic government has also found able exponents in America.[14] But it's a fact of government with which every First World country has had to deal, and for which no easy answer is forthcoming. The minutiae of governing must necessarily be delegated to people who won't always be faithful to their democratic masters.

Still, the problem is worse in America than in many other First World countries, and that's because we're too damn big. It's all very well to decry the managerial state, the regulatory excesses, but that's a problem of modernity generally. What makes it worse in the U.S. is that the government in Washington is more remote from ordinary Americans than, say, the government in Canberra is from ordinary Australians. The bigger the state, the easier it is for the special interests, the K Street lobbyists and the crony capitalists to capture the apparatus of government. That's why the administrative burden for Europeans became so much greater when the European Union began writing the rules, and why Brexit meant regulatory relief for Britons.

If secession isn't on the table, are we then supposed to throw in the towel? Representative government was neat, but now it's game over? Not quite. There's one more card to play, one suggested by Trump in his 2018 State of the Union address, and one played by Andrew Jackson with his spoils system: tell the disloyal bureaucrat that he's fired. And was that so bad? Dismissing holdover bureaucrats introduced a measure of political control over the government, and Jackson, in his 1830 address to Congress, argued that it would result in less corruption, not more. The bureaucracy had been captured by a self-interested elite with little concern for ordinary Americans, he said.

> Office is considered as a species of property, and government rather as a means of promoting individual interests than as an instrument created solely for the service of the people. Corruption in some and in others a perversion of correct feelings and principles divert government from its legitimate ends and make it an engine for the support of the few at the expense of the many.

Jackson's biographer, Arthur M. Schlesinger, Jr., concluded that the spoils system was a reform measure that helped restore people's faith in government, at a time when the bureaucrats had become a self-serving and unaccountable branch of government.[15] If that's what job tenure for bureaucrats has given us today, maybe it's time to reconsider it. At a minimum, expanding the number of political appointees who don't have job tenure, and who are always fired when a different party wins the White House, would be a sensible step.

Less radically, some of the administrative agencies might be moved from Washington to other parts of the country. The D.C. area is also one of the wealthiest in the country, and the proximity to the region's top employer helps produce the groupthink in which people march in ideological lockstep. Moving the agencies to other parts of the country might therefore serve to align their interests more closely with the country as a whole. I see no reason why the Department of Agriculture shouldn't be in Kansas, and I rather like the idea of resettling the regulators of the Environmental Protection Agency next to the unemployed coal miners of Harlan County, Kentucky.

LOBBYISTS

A regulatory reform commission and a return to the spoils system would go a long way toward draining the regulatory swamp. But what about the thousand-page bills that Congress writes, full of goodies sought by the crony capitalists and the lobbyists they employ? That's a subject for another book, one I've already written, as it happens. In *The Republic of Virtue*, I proposed several reforms that would weaken the hold that K Street lobbyists have over congressmen.[16]

Lobbyists usefully provide information about new and pending legislation to congressmen who often have little idea about what's before them. We'd not want to chill that, and constitutionally we can't. At the same time, there's no reason why lobbyists should also be allowed to contribute to congressional election campaigns. After the Jack Abramoff scandal, we banned overt gift giving by lobbyists to congressmen.[17] But when lobbyists sponsor campaign events, it's simply another form of gift giving, with all the earmarks of pay-for-play corruption, and this too should be banned.

For the same reason, congressmen and their senior aides shouldn't be permitted to work as lobbyists after they retire. A congressman can increase his salary from three to ten times as a lobbyist, and the Center for Responsive Politics reports that more than a third of the former members of Congress were registered as lobbyists or provided "strategic advice" for clients.[18] In the cynical view of one former representative, Congress has become a "farm team" for K Street.[19] And here's the problem: a congressman who expects to work for a lobbying firm will be at its beck and call, and when it wants something he'll be hard pressed to deny it.

BREAKING UP THE MONASTERIES

Andrew Breitbart was only half right when he said that politics is downstream from culture. Culture is also downstream from politics. If a country's culture shapes its laws, its laws also mold its culture. Causation works in both directions.

America doesn't have a minister of culture like France and most other countries. It does have a National Endowment for the Arts and a National Endowment for the Humanities, but these miniscule agencies are scarcely noticed by anyone other than the mutual back scratchers in the arts and the academy who apply for grants. Then there's Hollywood, a favorite bugbear of the Right. But since the studios are in the business of making money, they are consumer-driven and don't shape the culture so much as they are shaped by it. What else do we have? The foundations that qualify as educational charities; our colleges and universities; and now the "social media" giants. They all influence our political culture, even if they deny it.

Private Foundations. If a foundation doesn't overtly ask people to vote for or against a political candidate, its donors get a tax deduction. Foundations might be either "public" or "private." Public foundations solicit donations from the public, while private foundations do not. They are fully endowed by wealthy donors when they're set up, and don't need to find new donors thereafter. And that's a crucial distinction.

Public foundations are dependent on a steady stream of new donors, and in this respect they're consumer-driven, like Hollywood. That's not true of the private foundations that were funded by a megadonor generations ago, and they tend to abuse their discretion to advance tendentious political agendas that betray the donor's intent. Many of the biggest foundations, such as the Ford Foundation and the Pew Charitable Trust, were founded by donors with very conservative views, but over time they became major funders for left-wing causes. This pattern led John O'Sullivan, a conservative writer, to formulate O'Sullivan's Law: "All organizations that are not actually right-wing will over time become left-wing." In the first few years after the initial donation, the donor's appointees can be expected to respect his wishes, but after a while O'Sullivan's Law will typically kick in.

America's private foundations hold $1.5 trillion in assets.[20] Because they are allowed to spend their wealth in small amounts, they almost never spend it down, so they can be self-perpetuating. Lawyers will recognize the problem from their real estate classes on mortmain, which means that a "dead hand" is hanging on to wealth. Mortmain statutes were passed in the Middle Ages when English kings derived part of their revenue from inheritance taxes levied after a subject died. But those revenues were lost when land passed into the hands of a monastery, since it had perpetual existence. As a remedy, mortmain laws prevented the sale of land to a monastery without royal assent. Then, in the sixteenth century, Henry VIII and his grasping chancellor of the exchequer, Thomas Cromwell, dissolved the monasteries and confiscated their land and wealth. Problem solved.

America's private foundations are a new kind of monastery, calling for a new kind of mortmain law. No sensible person wants to play Henry VIII and seize private foundations' assets. But the foundations could be required to sunset their own existence. Senator Charles Grassley suggested that they should spend their assets more quickly, rather than sit on them forever. Alternatively, private foundations might be limited to a lifespan of, say, twenty-five years, during which time they would be required to spend down all their assets.[21] Such measures would put reasonable limits on their power to influence our culture in ways contrary to the intentions of their founders.

Higher Education. Many of our colleges and universities are deemed private foundations, and some have massive endowments. Princeton holds $2.6 million per student; Yale has $1.9 million; Harvard has $1.8 million. When a college is that rich, it needn't care overmuch about whether its students are acquiring useful knowledge; they will benefit from the institution's prestige in any case, and ambitious youth will still compete for the pricy advantage of a Harvard degree. That's one reason why so many elite schools have turned themselves into political indoctrination factories.

Liberals outnumbered conservatives in universities fifty years ago, but it was only by three to one. Now it's twelve to one, and in some fields, such as history, it's thirty to one. Nor is there any sign that the academy sees this as a problem. And it's only going to get worse, since the ratio of liberals to conservatives among newer academics is twenty to one. The conservatives who remain in higher ed are generally over sixty-five. They're aging out.

The thing that makes it worse is our student loan policies. Other countries, like us, offer state-supported loans for university students. But unlike us, they required the universities to cap tuition as part of the bargain. We didn't do so, and our private universities saw this as an excuse to run up the tab, increasing tuition fees far in excess of the rate of inflation. That's not a problem for the wealthy, or perhaps for the very poor who get a break on tuition. But it puts the top schools out of reach for middle-class families. This is not the case in other First World countries. Yearly tuition at the University of Toronto, Canada's best university, is US$3,500, while at Harvard it's $43,000. That's one reason why Canada is a mobile country and we're not.

In most other First World countries, the colleges are all pretty much the same. They're like Coca-Cola was for Andy Warhol back in the day. "What's great about this country," he said, "is that America started the tradition where the richest consumers buy essentially the same things as the poorest.... A Coke is a Coke and no amount of money can get you a better Coke than the one the bum on the corner is drinking. All the Cokes are the same and all the Cokes are good." The University of Toronto, the University of Saskatchewan, they're all about the same and they're all pretty good, so parents don't have to worry much about which school their child goes to. It's different in America, where there's a huge gap between the best and the worst colleges. The New Class sends its kids to elite schools, through "legacy admission" policies that favor the children of financial donors or by gaming meritocratic standards,[22] and that's what an aristocracy looks like.

Meanwhile, the burden of high tuition has made debt slaves out of many students from middle-class families. Debt loads in excess of $300,000 are not unheard of in America. That isn't a problem in Canada, where university tuition is much lower to begin with, and where students can burn off student debts in bankruptcy after seven years. Discharging student loans in bankruptcy is much harder to do in the United States since the Bankruptcy Code was amended in 1978.[23] Back then, tuition was pretty low and the assumption was that jobs would be waiting for graduates. Neither of those things is true today.

Of course, someone has to bear the loss if students can discharge educational loans in bankruptcy. And that should be the universities themselves, since they created the problem by jacking up tuition. This would give higher ed the incentive to keep costs down and to offer sensible courses that prepare students for employment, thus lowering the risk of default. Students enrolled in science, technology and engineering courses are safe bets to repay their loans. Those courses would continue to be offered, as would serious humanities courses. The students who take courses that provide little more than brainwashing in progressive politics are the most likely to find themselves unemployable and unable to pay debts. If an Evergreen State College persists in offering such courses and is held liable for student debt, it will teach itself into bankruptcy. It can't happen fast enough.

What about the super-rich universities, the ones that wouldn't worry so much about students defaulting? One worthwhile initiative, in the 2017 tax reform act, imposes a 1.4 percent tax on the endowment earnings of America's wealthiest universities, such as Princeton, Yale and Harvard. We wouldn't want to break them up, but a tax on investment earnings would serve to focus them on their educational mission. Were Thomas Cromwell around today, he might want to be a tax lawyer.

One more thing: when student mobs harass and threaten conservative speakers visiting the campus, our government should take notice. If racial minorities were the object of similar abuse, the federal Department of Education would cut off funds to a college. It's time to ask whether the same financial penalties should be meted out to institutions of higher education that punish faculty and students for their conservative beliefs.

Social Media. That leaves the social media giants such as Facebook and Twitter, Google and Amazon. Conservatives complain of their liberal bias, of the way in which they suppress conservative voices. Facebook happily paired with the Obama campaign in 2012, and more recently has banished Trump supporters. Twitter has banned some conservative provocateurs and "shadowbanned" others by suppressing their tweets. Some right-wing links seem to disappear quickly on Google, leading conservatives to try other search engines, and research conducted by Robert Epstein suggests they're not imagining this.

The enormously rich social media behemoths have employed their clout to influence tech-savvy intellectuals. When scholars at a liberal think tank defended the European Union's decision to impose a $2.7 billion antitrust fine on Google, they promptly got the boot after Google reminded the think tank who its donors were.[24] Google and other social media giants have also funded many of the antitrust and intellectual property academics, resulting in research projects uniformly tilted their way.[25] That's beginning to become a political issue. Both conservatives and the old-school liberals in the Bernie Sanders wing of the Democratic Party think the concentration of economic power in the social media giants undermines political freedom by constraining policy debates.[26]

Google and Facebook receive eighty-seven cents on every dollar of online advertising, and that's led to calls to break them up.[27] They're said to use unfair tactics to chill competitors, and along with the other social media giants they've been called "natural monopolies." A natural monopoly is a firm that operates in an industry where it's cheaper for a single company to provide services than for many companies to do so. When it comes to damming a river, for example, a single hydroelectric company can do the job at lower cost than two companies next to each other on the same river. Similarly, Facebook might be thought a natural monopoly because there's room for only one such network.

The legislature can't change the "natural" economic conditions dictating that there will be only one firm in the industry, but it can ensure that the one firm doesn't impose excessive monopoly prices on consumers. That's not a problem with Facebook, Twitter, Google or Amazon, since they're all free for consumers. The concern, rather, is that they'll use their market power to shape the political debate, promoting some kinds of speech and suppressing others.

That's something leftists used to worry about, but today it's a complaint you'll hear from conservatives. This is counterintuitive, since conservatives are ordinarily the last people to call for more regulations. Some of them have even wondered whether natural monopolies really exist.[28] In fact, the history of high tech offers reasons for doubt. In the 1990s, Microsoft was seen as a monopolistic threat to the high-tech industry and to democracy itself.[29] So the company was nearly split in two. But with the benefit of hindsight that looks foolish today. Microsoft's market share has fallen precipitously under competition with newcomers, especially to Android in smartphones. Among search engines, the once dominant Netscapes and CompuServes are melted away like the snows of yesteryear. In an ironic twist, Microsoft's Bing has been eating away at Google and now has 21 percent of the market share for search engines. In sum, it's all too easy—and wrong—to imagine that today's dominant firm, with all its first-mover advantages, will continue to dominate the market into the far future.

The case for busting up Google and the other social media giants is even weaker than it was for Microsoft twenty years ago. If you don't like Google, competition is only a click away, and nothing stops conservatives from starting their own social media platforms. If Facebook seriously silenced conservatives, for example, they could band together to form their own social network; and that possibility will likely keep Facebook more or less open to dissenting voices. As for Twitter, Donald Trump seems to have done well by it, even if he's not as popular as Justin Bieber. Moreover, if conservatives got into the game themselves, they might reasonably want to ban some of the same neo-Nazis and white nationalists that Facebook and Twitter do.

There's a more serious difficulty in asking politicians to regulate the social media giants with the idea of promoting political speech. That would be asking the swamp to regulate itself, and not just the swamp but the deepest of swamp dwellers, the politicians who try to silence political opponents. That was the story of the IRS scandal, where Democratic senators sought to persuade Lois Lerner to crack down on Tea Party organizations. That was also our experience with the "fairness doctrine," under which radio stations with a political message could lose their licenses unless they gave equal time to opposing viewpoints. Rather than court that risk, stations simply banned any one-sided political commentary. The Federal Communications Commission finally recognized that its policy had the result of suppressing political speech, and so it eliminated the fairness doctrine in 1987. It was only thereafter that we heard Rush Limbaugh.

We thought we had put paid to government efforts to shut down opposing voices, but it's a constant struggle. Now that Mark Zuckerberg has become everyone's favorite punching bag, we can expect Congress to try to regulate Facebook. In California, a Senate bill would require bloggers to employ fact checkers to stop the spread of false information,[30] and from there it's only a short step to regulating just who might serve as a fact checker. Fairness and truthfulness are all very well, but be careful what you wish for, especially when you ask the state to take on the swamp.

CHAPTER 12

HOW THE CONSTITUTION CREATED THE REPUBLICAN WORKERS PARTY

As we step back from the election, we recognize that we're prison-ers of a Constitution that makes a President Trump possible. It's not what James Madison wanted, but then we don't have a Madisonian constitution. What Madison wanted was something more like parlia-mentary government, with a president chosen by Congress. That, he thought, would filter out the unrefined outsider who might be chosen by an easily misled American electorate. And there's something to that. Filtration is what happens when British MPs choose the prime minister, and one can't easily see a Donald Trump on the government's front bench in Westminster.

A British prime minister must be more articulate than a George W. Bush, more clubbable than an Obama and more polished than a Trump. He must be able to rally his government on any of the issues of the day without a teleprompter, and do so with intelligence and wit. Madison's parliamentary president would have been up to this, but not many of today's American presidents. Bill Clinton might have come closest, though in a parliamentary system he would have been turfed out in 1998.

What the Framers of the Constitution agreed to, in place of filtra-tion, was Article II's complicated machinery for electing a president, and in the fullness of time this would come to mean popular election by the people. That gave America a series of estimable presidents—former governors, senators and military leaders. Earnest people, some a bit dull, but all well within the norms of a professional political class. Until we got to Trump.

What the voters expected from a president had evidently changed. Tastes always change, but two years ago they really did so, big league. By an order of magnitude, Trump is less concerned with public niceties than any president before him. But the real surprise is that it took so long to get to Trump. In 1952 we elected Dwight Eisenhower and our popular culture consisted of television programs like *The Ed Sullivan Show* and movies like *The Ten Commandments*. Compare that to the edgy groundbreakers and boundary pushers of today, the rap artists on Obama's playlist, the foul-mouthed comedians, and it seems a little precious to complain about Trump's demeanor. I can see how some people might object to Trump's manners, but wearing vagina-shaped hats in a march on Washington wouldn't seem the way to do so.

Liberals cheered the degradation of our popular culture, and then professed to be surprised when it spilled over into our politics. They shouldn't be. If they're upset, they're experiencing the rage of Caliban at seeing his face in the mirror.

Albert Camus would have recognized just how presumptuous Trump's critics are. He published *The Stranger* in Paris during the German occupation, a time of subjugation, compromise and collaboration; and the book's protagonist, Meursault, seemed devoid of empathy, a passive participant in life, a murderer. The book didn't take off at first, but after the war it became the must-read statement of French existentialism, and for a 1955 English translation Camus wrote a new introduction in which he called Meursault "the only Christ we deserve."

The secular reader took this as an expression of contempt for Christianity, even though Camus immediately said that he had not intended to blaspheme. As a student in North Africa, he had written a thesis about his compatriot, Saint Augustine, and though he didn't believe in God, Camus could never have been mistaken for a vulgar atheist. More sophisticated readers, such as Roger Shattuck, saw in the novel a defense of an ethic of authenticity, of fidelity to oneself, in which choices might be condemned as inauthentic but never as immoral.[1] There was at least one thing more that Camus might have meant, however, a comment not on God but rather on what "we" could be said to deserve, for Camus was an Augustinian without a sense of grace.

The NeverTrumpers, the outraged progressives assume that they're entitled to something better than a President Trump. But wherever did they get that idea? When I think on their venom, I rather wonder whether in Trump they have the only Christ they deserve.

There's another reason why Trump is a product of our Constitution, stemming from the constitutional separation of powers, the checks and balances that require the president, the Senate and the House of Representatives all to agree before a bill is enacted. This has given us a government without the reverse gear that's available in parliamentary governments, where a simple majority in the House of Commons can replace any law it wants. Macaulay thought that our government was all sail and no anchor, but it's turned out to be all anchor, so that wasteful laws prove impossible to repeal.[2] As far as bad ideas go, the separation of powers is up there with New Coke and Germany.

Until recently, the separation of powers did not prevent our two political parties from compromising over needed legislative reform. In the recent past, as many bills were passed in periods of divided government as when one party controlled all three branches of government.[3] That's because the two parties weren't as separated by ideological differences or by partisan animosities as they are today. But by the time of the 2010 midterm elections things had changed so much that from then until 2017, with Democrats in the White House and Republicans controlling Congress, it was understood that no major legislation could be passed.

What today's gridlock has given us is a constitutional crisis. There have been two previous constitutional crises, when constitutional fetters blocked necessary legislative changes. The first was the breakdown of government by the states under the Articles of Confederation, which the Framers corrected in 1787 by creating a proper federal government with our present Constitution. Even then, however, the federal government remained too weak and this resulted in our second constitutional crisis, one over slavery and resolved only by the Civil War, the Reconstruction Amendments and an enlarged federal government. We're now approaching a third constitutional crisis, where changes must be made and seemingly can't be made, where necessity is met with impossibility.

That's how Donald Trump became president. The 2016 election was a response to our constitutional crisis. Trump's supporters knew that a series of job-killing laws cried out for reform, that things were broken, that nothing would change unless we voted for the person who promised he was a change artist. We especially didn't want a nice guy who'd roll over when pushed by the Democrats.

Before changes can happen, however, we need to amend the way in which laws are passed. Trump has a major legislative agenda, but little of it can be enacted unless the Senate eliminates the need for a sixty-senator supermajority under its filibuster rules. That's a wholly imaginary barrier. Nothing really prevents the Senate, in any piece of legislation, from overriding the filibuster and passing a bill with a bare majority. Gridlock is already built into our Constitution, with the need for the House of Representatives, the Senate and the White House to get on board to pass a law, and the filibuster ratchets up the obstruction to an intolerable degree. It doesn't give us better government, but just the opposite. It blocks needed legislation and gives senators the power to extract wasteful earmarks.

So the Republican Workers Party has its work cut out for it. But if its goals seem so obvious, the question is how the New Class ignored it all. How did America's elite become indifferent to what most Americans wanted, to their welfare?

III

INDIFFERENCE AND GREATNESS

Among the delusions which at different periods have possessed themselves of the minds of large masses of the human race, perhaps the most curious—certainly the least creditable—is the modern soi-disant science of political economy, based on the idea that an advantageous code of social action may be determined irrespectively of the influence of social affection.

—John Ruskin, "Unto This Last"

CHAPTER 13

WHICH SIDE ARE YOU ON?

Something has happened to us, coarsened us, made us more uncaring. It's not something we saw happening, but one day we saw an unfamiliar face in the mirror. That's what moral decay is like. We discover with a start that we enjoy something that would have revolted us in our more innocent days, such as the voyeuristic thrill of reading J. D. Vance's *Hillbilly Elegy* or watching television series such as *Breaking Bad* and *Justified*, about a passively rotten working class that quite deserves our contempt.

Not that I have a problem with J. D. Vance. Rather, it's with the people who enjoyed his book.

REDNECK PORN

After the 2016 election, when white working-class voters turned out for Trump, the *New York Times* and the *Washington Post* sent their reporters to the hinterlands of Pennsylvania and West Virginia to see just what had happened. And off they went, like D.C. commuters sent horribly astray by a GPS that mistakes Buffalo for Bethesda, like cultural anthropologists dropping in on a particularly primitive society. That's how the *Post*'s Wesley Lowery came to spend a few days slumming in McDowell County, West Virginia. Lowery's editors had chosen well, for the county has the lowest life expectancy and the highest rate of drug-induced deaths in the United States. Males live an average of 63.5 years and females 71.5 years, while the national average is 76.5 for males and 81.2 for females. Between 1985 and 2013, the national lifespan increased

5.5 years for men and 3.1 years for women, but in McDowell County it declined 3.2 years for men and 4.1 years for women. The county gave 75 percent of its votes to Donald Trump.

McDowell's coal mines had closed, and the unemployment rate was more than double the nation's average. Without work, the county's young men got their kicks at a Friday night fight club where they tried to beat each other up in return for a chance at a prize. That was the subject of Lowery's story, one long sneer at his social inferiors.[1] "That $1,000, that's a whole lot of beer, man." The fights are scheduled just after the government welfare checks are delivered, which enables the spectators to buy their "$3 hot dogs drenched in warm chili." Between rounds, scantily clad ring girls dance for the crowd, with what Lowery unchivalrously described as "varying degrees of rhythm," and the reader was encouraged to enjoy observing their humiliation through photographs meant to make them look trashy.

Lowery's essay in redneck porn played to the prejudices of the *Post*'s readers. It invited them to hug themselves in self-delight for their social, educational and moral superiority, and reinforced their belief that the pollution-spewing coal-mining industry that Trump had praised deserved to die. It told its readers that the lower orders had brought their degradation upon themselves through their broken marriages, their illegitimate birth rates, their drug dependency, their general beastliness. And better still, it told its readers what to think of Trump voters in general.

Stories like that don't come out of the blue. The class divide they reveal has been around for a while. One famous example came after the rise of the Religious Right in the early 1990s, with televangelists such as Jerry Falwell and Pat Robertson. In 1993 the *Washington Post* heard the rumbles from the boonies and sent reporter Michael Weisskopf to visit the moonshiners, snake handlers and creationists and see what was happening. What he discovered was that the preachers had understood how to adapt to television, and that their followers were "largely poor, uneducated and easy to command."[2] The *Post* apologized the next day, but the story got Weisskopf shortlisted for a Pulitzer Prize.

Politicians are supposed to know better. And yet Obama let his guard down in 2008 when he asked himself why voters in economically depressed regions voted Republican. Very simple, he said. "They get bitter, they cling to guns or religion or antipathy to people who aren't like them or anti-immigrant sentiment or anti-trade sentiment as a way to explain their frustrations."[3] His chief rival, Hillary Clinton, quickly took him to task. But in 2016 she took the elitism one step further when she described Trump supporters as deplorables. Both candidates had committed the gaffe of telling us what they really thought about us.

In a way, Obama's condescension was more infuriating than Hillary Clinton's contempt. When Clinton tells you she despises you, she at least pays you the backhanded compliment of candid odium. Those who condescend, like Obama or David Brooks in the *New York Times*, are less honest. They profess a false sympathy while asking to be admired for their public display of concern. Here's Brooks, on the embarrassment of taking a member of the underclass to lunch.

> Recently I took a friend with only a high school degree to lunch. Insensitively, I led her into a gourmet sandwich shop. Suddenly I saw her face freeze up as she was confronted with sandwiches named "Padrino" and "Pomodoro" and ingredients like soppressata, capicollo and a striata baguette. I quickly asked her if she wanted to go some-where else and she anxiously nodded yes and we ate Mexican.[4]

If Brooks's friend read the *Times*, what do you suppose she would have thought of his betrayal?

Those who tell you of their contempt don't ask you to agree with them. Condescension is different. It asks you to accept your inferior-ity, as the obsequious Mr. Collins did in *Pride and Prejudice*. That's bad enough, but what really bothers Trump supporters about insolent, liberal condescension is the thought that their ostensible superiors aren't supe-rior in the things that matter most. True, they have their prestigious jobs, the prizes they give each other and all the marks of success the world can offer, but what if other things count, such as loyalty, kindness and piety? Saint Peter was merely a fisherman, and we have it on good authority that John the Baptist was not altogether tidy in his personal attire. But they had other things going for them. Cleverness isn't a substitute for goodness, and well-credentialed sepulchers can't be prettied up with a coat of white paint.

THE WRETCHED OF THE EARTH

People like Wesley Lowery invite readers to feel contempt for the white working class. But when Hillary Clinton called them deplorable, she meant something a good deal more hateful. "Racist, sexist, homophobic, xenophobic, Islamophobic, you name it," she said. Among the NeverTrumpers, even *National Review* agreed with her, with Jonah Goldberg telling us that the nationalism of Trump supporters came down to "white identity politics."[5] Racism, in short.

The media was only too happy to take up the bait, and this led to a search for the Great White Nazi, for which true white nationalists were only too happy to oblige. Emerging from under their pet rocks, a few moral lepers began to talk up white pride, and quickly found themselves in a symbiotic relationship with the Nazi-hunters in the liberal media. Here I am, said the racist, an authentic representative of the Trump movement. What think you of me!

For liberals, alt-right white nationalists became what Communists had been for the John Birch Society, a convenient tool to slander political opponents with conventional beliefs. The Birch Society's founder, Robert Welch, said that Dwight Eisenhower was a conscious agent of the Communist conspiracy. To which William F. Buckley responded: He's not a Communist, he's a golfer. Thereafter the John Birch crazies were consigned to the right-wing loony bin. Their equivalents today are the leftists who see Nazis and fascists everywhere. But no one on the left has tried to expel their own lunatic fringe, such as the so-called "antifascists" of Antifa. Instead, Welch's red-baiting tactics have been mimicked in hysterical smears by liberal pundits.

Ordinary conservatives found themselves portrayed as alt-right fascists. It became so unhinged that the charge of fascism was pinned on a conservative commentator who is an observant Jew and who had refused to vote for Trump. When Ben Shapiro planned to speak at UC Berkeley in September 2017 and Antifa protesters threatened a riot, the university sent a letter to students, faculty and staff offering counseling services for those who might feel threatened or harassed. Not by the Antifa rioters, mind you, but by the presence of a conservative speaker on campus. "We are deeply concerned about the impact some speakers may have on individuals' sense of safety and belonging," said the letter.[6]

A classic case of passive aggression, it suggested that university members were probably moral slugs if they weren't in need of counseling. For the occasion, the university fittingly closed off Sproul Plaza, the place where the Left's Free Speech Movement began in 1965.

Meanwhile, liberals had been writing puff pieces on Antifa thuggery.[7] "No enemies on the left" is what Alexander Kerensky said, and we know where that got him. No enemies on the left is what many liberals still think. But I had enemies on the right, the real neo-Nazis out there who had crawled out from under their rocks, and I wanted no part of them. In the fall of 2016, I organized a group of scholars and writers for Trump,[8] as much for the sheer perversity of the thing as for the support it would give the candidate. Surprisingly, it wasn't too hard to get people to sign aboard, a few courageous younger scholars, some emeritus professors who had nothing to lose, a careerist or two. What I didn't want were the alt-right types who might discredit the candidate, the white nationalists, the neo-Confederates, the people who thought that Marshal Pétain had gotten a bum deal. I wasn't going to have anything to do with them.

The charge that Trump voters were racists fell flat when so many counties flipped from voting for Obama in 2012 to Trump in 2016. There were twenty-two of them (out of seventy-two) in Wisconsin alone, the state that put Trump over the top. As for the gender gap, white women proved themselves traitors to their sex in 2016, and while more women voted for Hillary Clinton than for Trump overall, Clinton actually received a smaller portion of the women's vote than Obama had.

McDowell County in West Virginia also flipped from Democrat to Republican. It had given Obama 54 percent of its votes in 2008, but in 2016 Hillary Clinton got only 20 percent. Voters remembered her boast that, in pursuit of clean energy, "we're going to put a lot of coal miners and coal companies out of business."[9] Over in Harlan County, Kentucky, another coal-mining county a hundred miles up the road, people felt even more strongly about their jobs, and gave Clinton only 13 percent of their vote.

Harlan County is where the television series *Justified* is set, and it's sacred ground for the Left. It was the site of a bitter 1931 coal miners' strike that Pete Seeger sang about in "Which Side Are You On?" Written by a coal miner's daughter, the song described how Sheriff J. H. Blair tried to break up the miners' union.

> They say in Harlan County
> There are no neutrals there
> You'll either be a union man
> Or a thug for J. H. Blair
> Tell me, which side are you on, boys?
> Which side are you on?

There was a time when, in any class divide, we would instinctively side with the underdog, with the struggling families, the coal miners, the Joads in *The Grapes of Wrath*. We would have been ashamed to mock them, as Lowery had. But that was before we were instructed by our betters to despise them.

How different things were in the older literature of poverty. In 1936, *Fortune* magazine commissioned James Agee to report on the lives of three southern sharecropper families. The piece was never published, but it later became Agee's *Let Us Now Praise Famous Men*, the most celebrated account of Depression-era poverty. Agee took the assignment, and unlike Lowery he was sufficiently abashed to recognize the obscene voyeurism behind it. How curious it was, reflected Agee,

> to pry intimately into the lives of an undefended and appallingly damaged group of human beings, an ignorant and helpless rural family, for the purpose of parading the nakedness, disadvantage and humiliation of these lives before another group of human beings, in the name of science, of "honest journalism" (whatever that paradox might mean), of humanity, of social fearlessness, for money, and for a reputation for crusading and for unbias which, when skillfully enough qualified, is exchangeable at any bank for money.[10]

A generation later, Michael Harrington told us in *The Other America* that little had changed for the poor.[11] He brought his readers face to face with the hidden poverty in America, in the ghettos, sweatshops and small farms of America, and his book is credited as the inspiration for Medicaid and Medicare.

The earlier writers described the poor with compassion, as fellow Americans. At times the programs they proposed—the war on poverty—were ill-conceived, but there was no sense of moral superiority in this literature, even with those who might have brought their poverty on themselves. The desperately poor were broken in body and spirit, and while they didn't belong to anyone or anything, they still were our brothers, with whom we shared a common humanity and citizenship. If they lived their lives at a level beneath that necessary for human decency, we were called upon to do something about it. In Harrington's case, that had meant living with them in one of Dorothy Day's Catholic Worker hospices,[12] not an experience any of the purveyors of today's redneck porn will have shared.

TWO SOLITUDES

We've left the world of James Agee and Michael Harrington and entered a very different one. We've always been divided along racial lines, and it was a sign of moral progress to know that this was wrong. But today our class divisions are broader, and we've lost the sense that this is something of which we should be ashamed.

The members of the New Class have isolated themselves from the rest of America by the schools they attend, the movies and TV shows they watch, the restaurants where they dine. Cocooned in their "Super Zips," in D.C., New York, Los Angeles, San Francisco, they think they have earned their privileges and that those beneath them deserve their subordinate status. When they've bothered to think of those left behind, they've wondered why they can't be more like themselves. The conceit that the answer to the country's social ills lay in turning the working class into proper little left-wing intellectuals was wonderfully ridiculed by Thomas Frank in *Listen, Liberal*,[13] but somehow the New Class missed the satire.

The New Class lives in what Charles Murray calls the "bubble," a network of high-income people with similar educational backgrounds and cultural tastes. Theirs is a separate country, with little connection to the formerly encompassing institutions of schools, churches and military service that used to bring Americans together. If they happen to belong to a church, it's likely to be one where everyone shares the same political beliefs—in which case one might ask if it's actually a church. "All are welcome here," the signs announce. But what they mean is, "All are welcome here who think that all are welcome here."

If you're wondering whether you live in a bubble, here are some of Murray's test questions that might provide an answer.

- Have you ever lived for at least a year in an American neighborhood in which the majority of your fifty nearest neighbors did not have college degrees?
- Have you ever walked on a factory floor?
- Have you ever held a job that caused something to hurt at the end of the day?
- Have you ever had a close friend who was an evangelical Christian?
- What does the word "Branson" mean to you?

American class differences were starkly apparent in the 2016 election, with the geographical divide between the 487 counties Clinton won and the 2,520 ones Trump won. Most of Clinton's votes came from the East and West coasts, and there her support was so strong that she outpolled Trump by nearly three million votes in the entire country. Hers was the country of a bicoastal liberal elite, his of a conservative heartland, two solitudes that neither protect nor touch nor greet each other. America had become Disraeli's Britain, divided between two classes and two regions, between Two Nations,

> Between whom there is no intercourse and no sympathy; who are as ignorant of each other's habits, thoughts, and feelings, as if they were dwellers in different zones, or inhabitants of different planets.... The Rich and the Poor.[14]

Trump might have won many more counties, but that's not where the money was, or where the New Class lived. The counties Clinton won—only 16 percent of the total—accounted for 64 percent of America's 2015 economic activity.[15] That was a statistic that made Hillary Clinton and her fellow liberals feel smug. It shouldn't have.

The geographic concentration intensifies the polarization of

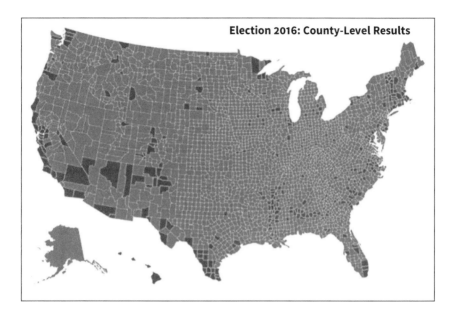

Election 2016: County-Level Results

County-Level Presidential Voting between Republicans ▪ **and Democrats** ▪

American politics. Over time, liberals become more liberal, conservatives more conservative. When everyone you know belongs to the same party, the instinct for moderation disappears, and when that happens, observed Robert Dahl, "the man of the other side is not just an opponent: he soon becomes an enemy."[16]

And that's what politics feels like, when you read the press or watch television. Sometimes I'd catch one of the late-night comedy shows, where audience members were invited to revel in their hatred of Trump. I couldn't watch for more than a few minutes, but that was long enough to wonder where the comedy might be. It seemed more like communal sadism, the laughter of the schoolyard bully who smacks his victim around. If it was supposed to be funny to depict Stephen Miller's head on a spike, as Stephen Colbert did on *The Late Show*, or to hold up the bloody head of a decapitated Trump, as Kathy Griffin would later do, then the anti-Semitic cartoons in the Nazi *Völkischer Beobachter* were a barrel of laughs. In the *Atlantic*, a shocked Caitlin Flanagan looked at our late-night television shows and asked, "*My God...What have we become?*"[17]

Flanagan's question was answered on June 14, 2017, when a left-wing gunman tried to kill Republican congressmen on a baseball field in Alexandria, Virginia. When that happens, there's only one criminal: the shooter. But it's still fair to ask whether he had listened to Ben Rhodes, who wished for the death of the Republican leadership. Or Sarah Silverman, who suggested that the military stage a coup against Trump. Or Madonna, who said, "I've thought a lot about blowing up the White House." Or CNN, which speculated about who would take over if Trump were assassinated on Inauguration Day. Or the *Washington Post* editorial board, which compared Trump to Hitler.[18] Or Hillary Clinton, who announced that she had joined the "resistance." She didn't meant it literally, of course, but the subtleties might have been lost on the gunman.

Now, with the tragedy in Charlottesville, where an anti-Trump protester was killed, each side has its victims, and each must learn to mistrust that most terrible of all delusions, the belief that, since one is virtuous, everything is permitted.

CHAPTER 14

THE PLEA OF IMPOSSIBILITY

Not so fast, says the liberal. We might want a more mobile country, but the fact is we can't get there. Because of things we can't change, we must remain immobile and unequal. We've moved to a high-tech, skills-biased economy that's created a permanent underclass, and nothing can be done about this. At the same time, we get to pat ourselves on our backs, since whatever advantages we enjoy come with the blessing of Mother Nature.

Something has taken the place of the idea of equality, something we had hoped we'd overcome, and it was the Great Chain of Being—the idea that we live in a universe where our position is fixed by nature and nature's god.[1] When people looked to theologians rather than scientists to make sense of a confusing world, the Great Chain of Being offered the comfort of a unified explanation of everything. From God himself at the apex down to mere earth below, all that is or could be had its established and immovable place. Below God there were hierarchies of angels, pure spirits; and below them man, both eternal spirit and fallible body. Lower still were soulless animals with the power of motion, and lower still were immobile plants with the power of growth. At the very bottom was matter, inert matter.

We thought the Great Chain of Being had been washed away by science. But we were wrong. As long as there are elites, there will be people who think they deserve their privileged status, that resistance is futile, that the underclass must accept its inferiority. And that's what many of our intellectuals right and left have come to believe. They themselves are skilled, and the unskilled must learn to suck it up in our new high-tech information economy.

We do indeed seem to be living in an age of rapid technological change. Movies from forty years back seem so clunky they're hard to watch. In *All the President's Men* (1976), Robert Redford playing Bob Woodward struggles through an old Minneapolis phone book to get the number of a former White House aide. Why don't you just Google him, we wonder. So it's all too easy to think that the loss of middle-class jobs can be blamed on skill-biased technological change (SBTC). We've moved to an information economy in which new technology favors highly skilled people in a high-tech world.[2] Low-skilled people, it's said, necessarily get left behind.

Yet technological change isn't exactly new. True, we have our cell phones and the Web, but technoskeptics have argued that there was more technological change in the early twentieth century, when telephones, automobiles, air travel, radio and electrification were introduced. If the pace of technological change has actually slowed, then SBTC theories wouldn't explain why we were mobile then but aren't today.

In addition, new technologies benefit low-tech as well as high-tech workers, and that's especially true of the industry that employed the largest number of American workers a hundred years ago: agriculture. At Farm Aid concerts, folksingers mourn the death of the family farm. Actually, the family farm is doing fine. What's happened is that it's gotten much bigger, thanks to technology.

The promise of a quarter section (160 acres) farm was enough to bring my mother's parents from Russia to Saskatchewan in 1909. On it they could raise a growing family, and a larger farm would have been hard to handle with the means then available. But by the time their sons signed up for the RCAF in 1939, a quarter section meant only subsistence farming. With the new tractors and harvesters, one-section farms—one square mile—had become the norm. Then the optimal size of farms exploded. In 1944, Massey-Harris introduced a self-driving combine, and by the time one of my uncles retired in the 1970s he had a farm of twenty-five sections—five miles by five miles in wheat, a little bit south of Saskatoon.

As the farms got bigger, the number of farmers got smaller, and the twentieth century saw a massive loss of agricultural jobs, displaced by new technologies. The number of farmers and farm laborers declined from 16 percent of the labor force in 1910 to 1 percent in 2000. At the same time, farming became more efficient: in wheat production, yield per acre tripled, while the yield per acre in corn increased by a factor of five.[3] SBTC isn't a new phenomenon, nor are the job losses that result from it.

What's different today is the absence of new jobs for those displaced by new technology. The boys who left the farms sixty and seventy years ago found new jobs in the cities, in manufacturing. In the case of my uncles, that meant the auto industry around Detroit and Windsor. But now the replacement jobs simply aren't there. Robots have moved onto the assembly line, and the lowering of trade barriers has shipped jobs abroad. Today the once prosperous towns in the rust belt have become what Trump, in the New York Economic Club, called the "silent nation of jobless Americans."

> Look no further than the city of Flint, where I just visited. In 1970, there were more than 80,000 people in Flint working for GM—today it is less than 8,000. Now Ford has announced it is moving all small car production to Mexico. It used to be cars were made in Flint and you couldn't drink the water in Mexico. Now, the cars are made in Mexico and you can't drink the water in Flint.

So you can see the appeal of SBTC theories. Nevertheless, they suffer from an embarrassing flaw once you realize that the countries that beat us in mobility aren't exactly living in the Stone Age. They have laptops in Denmark and cell phones in Canada. So technology doesn't look like a big part of the story. Something else is going on. It's that we were taught not to care about how others fared. We were taught indifference.

CHAPTER 15

THE ANATOMY OF INDIFFERENCE

The languages of liberty and equality, which establishment Republicans think so dissimilar, are not very different after all. In the Declaration of Independence, the self-evident truth of equality preceded that of liberty, and logically so, for the promise of liberty for some is hollow unless it means liberty for all. Otherwise, liberty might coexist with slavery, and that's how Abraham Lincoln skewered Stephen A. Douglas in their 1858 debate in Galesburg, Illinois: "I suppose that the real difference between Judge Douglas and his friends, and the Republicans on the contrary, is, that the Judge is not in favor of making any difference between slavery and liberty."

Once you say that a country can be half slave and half free, where do you stop? Why not 95 percent slave and 5 percent free? But if that's a free society, then a country might be free if only one man is free. That's what James I thought, when he entitled his defense of the divine right of kings *The True Law of Free Monarchies*. If the monarch was to be free, he could not be bound by anyone or anything, including Parliament.

That's not equality, or liberty either. And yet the two desiderata have been separated into watertight compartments. How did that happen, and how did we learn that equality doesn't matter? How were we taught indifference?

UNLEARNING EMPATHY

Is evil a moral or an intellectual failing? Actually, it's both, says Simon Baron-Cohen (Borat's cousin). It's blameworthy, but it's also a kind of cognitive error, one where we fail to understand what another person is feeling, or fail to understand how to act appropriately if we do. People who have that understanding are empathetic, and Baron-Cohen invites us to imagine evil as "empathy erosion."[1]

At a trivial level, the person who chats up the store clerk at the checkout counter might fail to consider the impatience of the long queue of shoppers behind her. And the grumbling people in line might themselves fail to consider that she may be a lonely person for whom this is one of the few human contacts she'll have that day. Both seem at fault, and the mistake seems to be an intellectual as much as a moral one. "What were you thinking?" we ask the person who's behaved badly.

Baron-Cohen is an academic psychologist, and he bolsters his arguments with pictures of the brain. Maybe it really is all about the size of the amygdala. That's what brain scans tell us, when psychopaths have been persuaded to get under the scanner. And perhaps we're also genetically predisposed to be empathetic or non-empathetic, as the case may be. But it's not either-or, says Baron-Cohen. Instead, people can be ranked along a bell-shaped curve according to their capacity for empathy, with low-empathy psychopaths on the left and moral heroes on the right. There are also gender differences, with males to the left (relying more on abstract rules) and women to the right (more conscious of others' feelings).[2]

It's not all about genetic differences, however, or even solely about one's ability to read what other people are feeling. People on the autism spectrum can be caring individuals, even if they lack the intellectual ability to recognize pain in others. They might not see it, but if you tell them that someone is upset, they'll feel upset too. They can also be trained to improve their social skills, for example to look people in the face and not in the ear when they talk to them.

If empathy erosion can be reversed through moral education, might empathy also be unlearned? Could a normally empathetic person be taught to ignore his feelings and act in a callous manner? When you look at American politics with its free-range hatreds, the Antifa thugs, the alt-right monsters, the answer is obviously yes.

Callousness can be taught, when we're instructed that some people don't deserve much consideration. They might be the slaves of Jefferson's time or the deplorables for Hillary Clinton. They might also be blamed for bringing their ills upon themselves, as NeverTrumpers have charged. In all these ways, empathy erosion is permitted, even encouraged. One of the most delicious of human emotions is the sense of justified hatred, and empathy erosion gives it a permission slip.

In a hyperlegalistic society, such as the United States, we can also unlearn empathy when legal norms substitute for moral ones. Today when someone says "that's just wrong!" what he often means is "there ought to be a law." The moralist imagines himself to be a legislator, and constitutional law is our higher morality.

What purely legal norms miss is the complexity of moral decisions, and that was what Grant Gilmore meant when he said that in Hell there will be nothing but law.[3] It was also the point behind Lawrence Kohlberg's famous example of an ethical dilemma. Suppose a pharmacist has discovered a cancer-curing drug. While it costs only $200 to manufacture, he refuses to sell it for anything less than $2,000. The drug would save the life of a woman who is dying of cancer, but her husband can't scrape together more than $1,000 to buy it. He tells the pharmacist that he needs the drug for his wife, and asks if he can buy the drug for that amount. "No," says the pharmacist. "It's my property and I can sell it for what I want."[4] Kohlberg's hypothetical was vividly evoked in 2015 when Martin Shkreli, a hedge fund manager, bought the property rights to a life-saving drug and then raised the price of a pill from $13.50 to $750. It looked outrageous, but there's nothing wrong with that if you're a property rights absolutist.

In such a case, what would a man be ethically justified in doing to save his wife? How should others judge him if he decided that the only option was to steal the life-saving drug? Kohlberg asks people to choose between a narrow legal response (theft is illegal) and a more complex understanding of moral dilemmas, in which the value of a life might trump the pharmacist's property rights. The person who is inclined to justify theft in this situation shows a higher moral development than one who sees it simply from a legal perspective, said Kohlberg. Turning moral problems into legal ones can make a stone of the heart and anesthetize our sense of empathy.

Kohlberg's hypothetical was anticipated in *Les Misérables*, where Jean Valjean is condemned to five years in the galleys for stealing a loaf of bread to feed his starving family. It is also the moral behind the scene in which Inspector Javert asks Sister Simplice whether she is hiding Jean Valjean—the story that made a Communist of Whittaker Chambers.[5] "Are you alone in the room," asks Javert. Yes, says Sister Simplice—even though Valjean is hiding in the corner. "Have you seen Valjean?" No, says the nun. Two quick lies, one after the other, from one who had never lied before. "O holy maiden," writes Hugo. "May this falsehood be remembered to thee in Paradise." Well yes, replies the legalist, but let's not forget that the good nun was guilty of obstruction of justice and lying to an officer of the law, and while we might think French penal law unnecessarily harsh, we shouldn't wish to condone theft.

CONSERVATIVE INDIFFERENCE

Conservatives unlearned empathy in five ways. First, conservatism was captured by the economists, with the flashy new tools they brought to their discipline in the twentieth century. We'll give you an intellectual rigor you've been lacking, they said, but along the way they also ditched the concern for spreading the wealth around. Second, some conservatives became prisoners of abstract theories of natural rights that tell us what is owed to ourselves and don't pay overmuch attention to the welfare of others. Third, some subscribed to "moral poverty" explanations of social pathologies that blamed the victim for his misery. Fourth, the conservative snob is not apt to care how the other half lives. Finally, the heroic materialism that defines the deepest beliefs of many conservative thinkers celebrates the pagan virtues at the expense of sympathy for the poor in spirit, the meek, they that mourn.

This doesn't describe ordinary conservative voters, mind you, but only the Perfect Republican Idiots who pass themselves off as the movement's thinkers, the writers for the little magazines, the priesthood of intellectuals who formed the NeverTrump movement and who were left in the dust by their failure to understand lay Republicans.

Economism. Nineteenth-century economists assumed that we pretty much knew what people wanted, and concentrated on their material welfare. Do people have enough food, are there jobs for them?[6] Along came the twentieth century, and the economists found they could dispense with a lot of those earlier assumptions, especially the idea that we know anything about what other people want, except as measured by what they buy. If that's so, we have no basis for any judgments about social justice.[7] How can I design a social safety net, when other people look like zombies to me?

That might have been an appropriately modest assumption for a social scientist who wants to seem scientific, but the scientist oversteps his bounds when he tries to tell us how to live. His academic modesty then becomes an excuse for a heartless welfare regime. And there is no reason to credit him with moral insight. If he were right, we wouldn't be able to say whether the wealth transfer should be from the rich to the poor or vice versa, and we all know better than that. If he were right, we wouldn't have a clue how to make our own personal gifts to charity. And yet the false economism had a fatal charm for a generation of tightwad conservative thinkers.

Once again, I'm not talking about Americans in general, who give more to charity than people in other countries. I'm not even talking about ordinary conservatives, since people in Republican states give more than people in Democratic states.[8] Instead, I'm referring to a conservative intellectual class whose anti-welfare policies rest on an esoteric and misleading economic foundation.

Natural Rights. Second, conservative natural rights theorists can too easily unlearn empathy by turning moral questions into legal ones. They're the captives of "rights talk," of the idea that political and moral issues come down to natural rights legally owed to oneself, and they don't have much room for a Sister Simplice in their moral vocabulary. One part of their moral sense expands like a tumor and crowds out that part which asks what is owed to others, and what a sense of empathy would ask of one.

That's not to deny the appeal of natural rights, which very properly play a role in our moral discourse. A society is to be judged in part on whether it respects democratic rights and the right to practice one's religion. But with a sense of empathy, we'd also care about how other people fare, about the consequences of adhering to a set of rights.

Often there's no conflict. A respect for natural rights usually does make most people better off, as compared to the experience of people in failed socialist states such as Venezuela. There's also no reason in theory why doctrines of natural rights can't make room for a robust sense of duties to others. John Locke advanced the best-known defense of natural rights, one that greatly influenced America's Founders, yet he also saw a God-given sense of sociability as a ground for duties to others, where these do not conflict with self-preservation.[9] But for too many conservatives, the language of rights became paramount and numbed the concern for how things worked out in practice for other people.

When Mitt Romney distinguished between "makers" and "takers," he suggested that the former deserved their fortune and that the latter were owed nothing. For some on the right, such as the followers of Ayn Rand, that's a foundational belief. They adhere to a heartless ideology and deserve the same rebuke that Flannery O'Connor gave to Mary McCarthy. O'Connor had been invited to a chic New York dinner party, meant to introduce the Catholic novelist to New York intellectuals. But McCarthy dominated the conversation, and O'Connor remained silent until late in the evening. Finally someone realized that the guest of honor had not spoken and, in an effort to draw her out, mentioned the Catholic doctrine of transubstantiation, the transformation of bread and wine to the body and blood of Christ. Of course it's just a metaphor, said McCarthy, a lapsed Catholic; but it's a beautiful metaphor. "If it's just a metaphor, to Hell with it," answered O'Connor. If it's a natural right and doesn't leave people better off, to Hell with it.

Blaming the Victim. The third reason for the loss of empathy, for why conservatives had become indifferent to what had happened to lower- and middle-class Americans, was that they had learned to blame the victim. If the lower orders had sunk into poverty, if their children weren't getting ahead, it was their own damn fault.

This was taken from an older playbook, in the conservative's reaction to the plight of the black underclass. In the 1965 Moynihan Report, black poverty was blamed on the decline of two-parent families. The Aid to Families with Dependent Children (AFDC) program didn't make pay- outs to mothers if a man was in the house, and not surprisingly this led to a rise in single-parent households.[10] Then, in *Losing Ground*, Charles Murray reported that the black unwed birth rate had skyrocketed, from

24 percent for black infants (and 3.1 percent for white infants) in 1965, to 40 percent for black infants (and 12 percent for white infants) in 1985.[11] The AFDC had played a role in this, but people began to think that it wasn't so much about economics as it was about moral decay, about a generation of fatherless super-predators. In a highly influential 1995 article, John DiIulio, a sociologist at Princeton, advanced a "moral poverty" explanation of what had changed.

> Moral poverty is the poverty of being without loving, capable, responsible adults who teach you right from wrong. It is the poverty of being without parents and other authorities who habituate you to feel joy at others' joy, pain at others' pain, happiness when you do right, remorse when you do wrong. It is the poverty of growing up in the virtual absence of people who teach morality by their own everyday example and who insist that you follow suit.[12]

Among some conservatives, the language of virtue trumped economics, and their leading thinkers began to sound less like Milton Friedman and more like Cotton Mather. The "virtuecrats" looked at Bill Clinton's shenanigans, and bemoaned the decline in private morality. How different the American Founders were, they said, and took to quoting James Madison. "To suppose that any form of government will secure liberty or happiness without any virtue in the people is a chimerical idea."[13]

There were two problems with the moral poverty theories, however. First, they predicted that things could only get worse, that with the rise of unwed births the inner cities would become abandoned to gangs of feral youths, but this didn't happen. Instead, crime rates went down, as youthful offenders confronted economic realities in the form of stiffer criminal penalties. Second, none of this explained the difference in the black and white rates of crime and unwed birth, unless one wanted to wade into the swamp of black-white differences. Apart from out-and-out racists, no one wanted to go there, but both conservatives and liberals were content to let the question linger.

That's where things stood thirty years ago. A 40 percent unwed birth rate for black Americans in 1985 was distressingly high, but when Charles Murray wrote *Coming Apart* in 2012, the unwed birth rate for blacks had nearly doubled, to 70 percent. The bigger news, however, was the tenfold increase in the white unwed birth rate, from 3 percent to 30 percent. There was a similar increase in the white divorce rate and a decline in the white marriage rate. There was also a growing drug dependency, especially for opioids such as OxyContin.

Racists who had blamed black unwed birth rates on African American moral poverty now had to confront the shockingly high white unwed birth rates. And that's when the NeverTrumpers discovered the silver lining in Murray's findings. The pathologies of the white under-class gave them a twofer. It explained the rise in income immobility, as well as that insidious threat to all we hold dear: the Trump phenomenon. Trump had argued that America's lower classes had been harmed by ter-rible schools, immigration and crony capitalism, but that was all wrong, said the NeverTrumpers. Rather, the poorest of whites had simply copied the immiserating cultural norms of a black underclass, and that's why they were immobile. It's also why they turned to Trump. In *National Review*, Kevin Williamson wrote that "the white American underclass is in thrall to a vicious, selfish culture whose main products are misery and used heroin needles. Donald Trump's speeches make them feel good. So does OxyContin."[14]

The NeverTrumper's indifference to the working class, white and black, seemed especially callous after we learned what had happened to mortality rates. We've come to expect that people will live longer than ever before, with new drugs and better medical providers. We're saving people who in the past would have died earlier from things like heart disease and cancer. That's how it is in every other First World country, and that's how it is for African Americans and Hispanics in this country. But life expectancy rates for white Americans have recently declined. Anne Case and her husband, Sir Angus Deaton, a Nobel laureate, reported that if the rate had held at 1998 levels, there would have been 100,000 fewer deaths over the next fifteen years for whites ages 45–54. The deaths were concentrated in economically depressed parts of the country, in places like Appalachia. Life expectancy there is lower today than in Bangladesh.

You can see it all on the FiveThirtyEight website. For the white working class, the increased deaths are, importantly, a result of the dis-eases of despair, social isolation, drug and alcohol poisonings, suicide and chronic liver disease.[15] White working-class Americans were killing themselves, but they're doing it to themselves, said the NeverTrumpers; while social justice warriors at our elite colleges were asking them to check their privilege and Hillary Clinton was calling them deplorable and irredeemable.

The NeverTrumper had assumed that the white working class had lost their jobs because they smoked Oxy, because of moral poverty. But there's another explanation. Maybe they smoked Oxy because they had lost their jobs. Maybe it was really about economics after all, and not a sudden loss of virtue. That's what Case and Deaton think, and the American counties with the highest death rates from mental disorders and substance abuse are the counties with higher unemployment rates and fewer prime-age males in the labor force.[16] A 2.6 percent increase in a county's unemployment rate over a year-2000 baseline is associated with a 29 percent increase in suicides and an 84 percent increase in accidental poisonings.[17]

In the 1980s, William Julius Wilson gave the same economic explanation for the higher black unwed birth rate. Black families were weaker than white ones because black unemployment levels were much higher than those for white families, particularly in the inner cities from which jobs had vanished. Add to that the racial and cultural prejudices of white employers, and it's not hard to see why black unemployment rates were double those of whites. As a consequence, black families were more dependent than whites on welfare checks, and thus more likely to be affected by welfare's perverse incentives.[18]

We're not going to be able to say which came first, the job loss or the Oxy, but if it's solutions we're after they'll not come from a moral rearmament crusade. A state that wants to wean people from opioids might want to regulate their use, but in the end the best inducement to moral living is a good job. From that will follow marriage, mortgages and children, all the things that make us moral. Trump said he wanted to be remembered as the jobs president, and if he succeeds, for both whites and blacks, the drug crisis will take care of itself. What's not going to be of any help to anyone is the heartless conservatism that blames the victims.

The Dandy. There's a further reason why conservatives stopped caring about middle-class America. They are fond of tracing their ideas back to Thomas Jefferson or Abraham Lincoln, but sometimes there's a bit of the elegant John Randolph of Roanoke in them as well. Or so they wish. "I am an aristocrat," said Randolph. "I love liberty. I hate equality."

Dandies like Randolph, or like Charles Baudelaire, Maurice Barrès and Oscar Wilde, made a cult of themselves, of their originality in the face of banal mediocrities and unspeakable barbarians. They sought, by their example, to be a living reproach to all that was second-rate and tawdry about them. Similarly, the American dandy will seek to signal his superiority to the common herd. He'll thrill to read about John Randolph swaggering into the House of Representatives with his riding crop and pack of dogs, and he'll try to mimic William F. Buckley's English accent, his ostentatious display of verbal theatrics, his arrogant dismissal of political opponents (though perhaps not his piety). "Some people stoop to conquer," said Buckley. "I just conquer."

Buckley is credited with rescuing conservatism from the doldrums of Eisenhower-era Republicanism. On college campuses fifty years ago, young conservatives dressed like dandies and affected an exaggerated vocabulary and a mid-Atlantic drawl. None of them tried to pass themselves off as the second coming of Senator Everett Dirksen (R-IL). In time, most grew out of their stylish affectations, but the appeal to snobbism had a lasting influence that wasn't entirely healthy, for it cuts one off from the concerns of ordinary Americans.

Heroic Materialism. Whether he takes his cues from Aristotle or Nietzsche, or mediated through people such as Allan Bloom and Ayn Rand, the conservative who prizes the pagan virtues, the great-souled over the small-souled man, excellence at the expense of mediocrity, might have good taste, but is nevertheless apt to have a low opinion of *pauvre humanité*.[19] With more candor such people might confess their contempt for the Sermon on the Mount; and concede that, like Nietzsche and the French New Right philosopher Alain de Benoist, they are anti-Christian at heart. But they're more inclined to veil their deepest beliefs by speaking of their "esoteric" learning. Now you know what that means.

It's an intellectual thing. Such people are apt to regard religion in general, and Christianity in particular, as philosophically uninteresting. And I expect they're right. But I am more interested in what religion adds, for there's nothing wrong with Aristotle, or with liberalism for that matter, that the Judeo-Christian tradition wouldn't cure.

In all these ways—economism, natural rights theory, blaming the victim, dandyism, heroic materialism—conservative intellectuals were taught indifference. And yet, in his personal giving, the conservative is apt to be generous, and argue that private charity effectively compensates for public meanness. Mind you, unless he is an anarchist, the conservative won't make the same argument about how the rest of the government might be funded. We're not going to be asked to pay for our aircraft carriers from voluntary contributions. The conservative is also understandably skeptical about our frequently wasteful social welfare programs. If yesterday's liberals sought to promote equality, they sometimes tried too hard. But today's liberals have also learned indifference, just like the conservatives.

LIBERAL INDIFFERENCE

In the past, liberals prided themselves on their empathy, but now they're all too ready to ridicule middle-class voters, to call them deplorable. Or to think them stupid. That was the point of Thomas Frank's *What's the Matter with Kansas?* Were they not so thick, said Frank, the solidly Republican voters of Kansas would vote for "the party of the workers, of the poor, of the weak and the victimized."[20] The Democrats, in other words. Instead, the Kansans stupidly backed Republican candidates who spoke to unimportant social issues such as abortion.

With greater self-knowledge, Frank would have asked, "What's the matter with liberals?" They had boasted of their concern for the little guy, while supporting education, immigration and economic policies that had created an immobile class society. After the 2016 election, they hinted that they might be ready to admit the white working class as a new, privileged identity group (for that is the only way in which liberals solve social problems), but without abandoning the policies that had kept them immobile. If anyone was stupid, it was they, for when Trump addressed the Kansan's economic as well as his social concerns, he had an answer for Frank. Nothing is the matter with Kansas—now.

The liberals were not as smart as they had thought. Mostly, however, they were not as compassionate. They had given up on solidarity, on their bonds to fellow citizens. They no longer cared about equality. And that's new. In the past, two currents of left-wing thought would have regarded equality as a moral imperative, as demanding something from us: Marxism and egalitarian liberalism. But today, neither is up to the job.

Marxism. Marxism never really preached true equality, but only a solidarity with one class, the workers. Other classes, the kulaks, the capitalists, deserved nothing. Equality before the law was a false ideal that entrenched a dominant propertied and capitalist class, and served bourgeois class interests which themselves were rooted in inequalities. In place of bourgeois equality, Marx and Engels proposed the abolition of class society, which would be followed by communism's authentic equality. Pyotr Tkachev, "the first Bolshevik," explained how this would happen: the revolution would abolish all the elites, and it would be carried out by a revolutionary elite.

The Marxist dream of universal brotherhood and a class-free world has died, in the moral and political bankruptcy of communism. Among the progressive Left it has been abandoned for identity politics that explicitly deny a common humanity by granting priority to favored groups—minorities, gays, women. Yesterday's kulaks are today's white men.

Identity Politics. There was a telling moment in a Democratic presidential debate on CNN in 2015, when the candidates were asked to choose between "Black Lives Matter" and "All Lives Matter." One might have thought that only a moral imbecile or a racist would judge people by the color of their skin and not by the content of their character. Have we come that far from Martin Luther King's "I Have a Dream" speech? But among the candidates, only Jim Webb said that all lives matter, and he left the Democratic Party not long afterward.

In the past, identity politics was more benign and traveled under the label of "pluralism." America was composed of separate voting blocks and interest groups, said the pluralist: the Irish, the National Association of Manufacturers, southern segregationists, the sugar lobby, the Jews, the blue-collar unions, and together the crazy quilt constituted a winning Democratic coalition. It was messy, but the pluralist allowed himself to believe that somehow, from the competition for political influence, the best overall policies would emerge. In fact, pluralism required a good deal of cognitive dissonance and lived in a swamp of crony capitalism and pay-for-play corruption, but at least it purported to seek the greatest happiness of the greatest number. It didn't go around looking for people to blame. Today's identity politics are very different, however. The sunnier ways of pluralism have been abandoned for the darker and more thrilling search for Enemies of the People.

Trump's election pitilessly ripped off the mask of compassionate liberalism and revealed the secret contempt that lay hidden behind a rhetoric of empathy. It also showed that today's liberalism lacks a stopping point, the sense that things might be carried too far. Taking identity politics to its logical conclusion, a blogger recently suggested disenfranchising white men for twenty years, to "strike a blow against toxic white masculinity."[21] That turned out to be a parody of the Left's primitive tribalism, but it was sufficiently close to the progressive mainstream to be accepted for posting by the HuffPo editor. Nor was it far removed from a proposal in the *Washington Post* that black Americans be given 5/3 of a vote to make up for past racial injustices.[22] To do so, of course, we'd have to get over some ideas that used to be modern, such as the constitutional hang-up about one person, one vote.

Our Rawlsian World. Egalitarian liberalism got a boost from John Rawls in *A Theory of Justice*.[23] But while Rawls began from an egalitarian foundation, he derived tendentious conclusions that serve to reinforce class distinctions. To get started, he borrowed the "maximin" strategy from game theory, in which players maximize the minimum outcome available to them. For example, suppose there's a choice between two job offers, one with a sure-thing annual salary of $50,000, and another with a 50 percent chance of $160,000 and a 50 percent chance of $40,000. A player who's comfortable with risk would take the second job, with its higher expected payoff of (.5 × $160,000 + .5 × $40,000 =) $100,000. The maximin player doesn't like risk, however, so he'll go with the guaranteed annual salary of $50,000.

Rawls then argued that a theory of justice must link the maximin strategy to a concern for the worst-off among us. This was his *difference principle*, under which economic inequalities are unjust if the very poor can be made materially better off. If this seems right, that's because it rests upon our moral intuition that the poor are especially worthy of our concern. It's also the teaching of the Jewish-Christian Bible, the command to attend to the needs of widows and orphans, the message that "as long as you did it to one of these my least brethren, you did it to me" (Exodus 22:22; Matthew 25:40). In the Catholic Church, it's called the preferential option for the poor.[24] No hint of any religious doctrine is to be found in *A Theory of Justice*, however. Rawls expressly denied that his ideas depended on our moral or religious intuitions, which he regarded as hopelessly imprecise.

Yet the difference principle is not a model of precision itself. For if we're supposed to pay the closest attention to the least well-off, just who are they? Are they the bottom 10 percent of earners, the bottom 1 percent or simply the absolutely worst-off person we can find? The economist Thomas Sowell mocks Rawls by imagining the worst-off person as the wino on the street corner. If that's who it is, and every political scheme is to be judged on whether it makes him better off, the difference principle becomes what Sowell called "the wino's veto."

That's rather harsh, mind you. It is possible to give content to the difference principle without completely specifying the members of the least well-off class. When Christ spoke about my least brethren, he wasn't called on to say, "Now, let's be clear about this." As Rawls insisted, it's politics, not moral geometry, and politics can be rough at the edges. So let's say the poorest class is the bottom 10 percent. The problem is that the absolute priority that the difference principle accords to the least well-off ignores the welfare of those a notch up, and these were the Trump supporters. To take their concerns properly into account, one would have to adopt a more encompassing criterion of justice, one that looks at how people generally fare,[25] across different economic classes, and that's just what the difference principle doesn't do.

The difference principle has become the unofficial ideology of our immobile, class-ridden society. It gives a pass to the top 10 percent so long as the bottom 10 percent are well provided for. "There is no injustice in the greater benefits earned by a few," said Rawls, "provided that the situation of persons not so fortunate is thereby improved."[26] So Rawlsian liberalism, though ostensibly revolutionary, is really a very complacent theory of justice that preaches indifference and tells the New Class it can keep its privileges.

And that's how it's turned out. We live in a Rawlsian world, one with a privileged top 10 percent and a very generous welfare system for the bottom 10 percent, but with stagnation and job losses for those in between. For the wealthy trial lawyer, the media star, the financial executive, the price to be paid for a clear conscience is political support for a party that makes it its business to proclaim its support for the very poorest among us—the devil take those just above them. All the same, the idea that embracing progressive politics might give the well-to-do a pass is something that puzzled the philosopher G. A. Cohen, who asked, *If You're an Egalitarian, How Come You're So Rich?*[27]

Political differences don't always bring out the warmest of feelings, but all the same there's a callousness in today's American politics that we've not seen since the Civil War. On both the right and the left, the bonds of equality and fraternity have been frayed to the breaking point. In the past, there was something to remind us of our ties to each other, something that isn't there anymore. What was it, then?

CHAPTER 16

PASCALIAN MEDITATIONS

There's a stereotype about the French. They're hyperrational, theoretical, rule-driven, we think. The French themselves are also apt to see things that way, when they describe themselves as Cartesian. But there's another, more skeptical philosophical tradition in France, one that owes little to rationalism or to René Descartes, and that can be traced to Blaise Pascal and his distinction between the Cartesian spirit of geometry and the "spirit of finesse." In our choices, said Pascal, we often arrive at the proper ends (*fins*) immediately, instinctively and intuitively, through hunches that substitute for calculation.[1] That was how Victor Hugo's Sister Simplice decided to shelter Jean Valjean, and it's how Albert Camus broke with the Stalinist Left. They were Pascalians.[2]

Until the new field of behavioral economics arose and garnered a string of Nobel prizes,[3] there was really nothing like a Pascalian intellectual tradition in the United States. American constitutional conservatives thought that the Framers had given us a brilliant machine that would go by itself and produce nothing but the wisest legislation. We would enact only the best of laws, and would never need the reverse gear that parliamentary systems so easily employ. The utilitarians thought it came down to measuring pleasures and pains in a felicific calculus. The natural rights theorists thought that it could all be worked out from first principles. The Rawlsians told us that justice was a kind of moral geometry. They all sought the rock of a good, hard theory. The Cartesian republic isn't France. It's America.

As a child in public school, I was taught a very different lesson and became a Pascalian. One day an imbecilic, hydrocephalic boy was brought to class. He could not talk, but from the way he smiled he seemed very happy to join us. I imagine his parents felt the experience would be good for him, and that our teachers—the Sisters of Charity— thought the experience would be good for us.

I'd like to report that his fellow students befriended him, but we didn't. We were six or seven years of age, a little shy and formal, and perhaps worried that we would open ourselves to ridicule if we approached him. No one mocked him, but no one sought him out either. He lasted no more than a week among us, and I never knew what happened to him, but since then not a year has passed when I've not recalled him. I can see his face, but count it a shame that I can't remember his name.

What the experience taught me was that moral choices require right instincts more than right reason, and that we're more likely to learn them from Victor Hugo than from political metaphysicians. It's also why I was never tempted to join the NeverTrumpers. They had all the clever theories, the economism, the natural rights principles, the libertarianism, but we Trump supporters saw things they had missed. The NeverTrumpers had what W. B. Yeats described in "The Seven Sages" as a "rancorous, rational sort of mind, that never looked out of the eye of a saint, or out of drunkard's eye." We for our part understood that wisdom might come from an idiot's smile.

The Sisters of Charity had a special reverence for the Curé d'Ars, Saint Jean-Marie Vianney, a French priest of the early nineteenth century who served as the model for the clerical novels of Georges Bernanos. The Church has had a good many highly intelligent saints, but the Curé d'Ars wasn't one of them. He was mentally slow and scarcely able to master the Latin he needed to become a priest. He was, however, a profoundly holy person, and it was that combination of sanctity and simplicity that commended him to the nuns. The sisters gave us relics of his cassocks and encouraged us to share their love for his simple gifts.

In his time, the Curé d'Ars was venerated by his parishioners as a saint, and even people of other religions recognized his holiness. One day he came across a Protestant lady, and in his gentle way he remonstrated with her: Madame, you are a profoundly good person, he said, but tell me where was your Christ when you left the Church? "He was in the hearts of people like you, M. le Curé."

I mention these little stories to emphasize how deeply perverse they might seem to the modern reader (for all this happened many years ago). Worth today is measured on an IQ scale, not a holiness one. Indeed, the very idea of holiness will seem unintelligible to most people, the idea that merit attaches to a life devoted to the service of God, quietly, humbly lived in a little village, without television screens to celebrate public displays of virtue. As for my hydrocephalic classmate, many will think it a shame he was not aborted. But then I would have missed his message about the sanctity of life, of all life. And he would have missed his life, which I expect had more moments of holiness than mine ever will.

I have another reason to mention my experience at school, for I want to distinguish the radical equality that the Sisters of Charity embraced from the divide between the makers and takers of Mitt Romney and the American Enterprise Institute, between Big and Little Brains. I thought my hydrocephalic classmate had presented me with a moral challenge (which I had failed), but I suspect that intellectuals on the right would think this mere sentimentality. Here's Bryan Caplan, a George Mason economist, warning us against sympathizing with the slow-minded.

> Are low-skilled Americans the master race? Economists are used to rolling their eyes when people object to better policies on the grounds that some special interest will suffer from the change. It's time to cross the final frontier, and start rolling our eyes when the special interest is low-skilled Americans.[4]

The economist can tell us how to choose rationally, in order to advance our own interests. What he can't do is teach us empathy or fraternity. He might explain how to build a society in which I and others might flourish, through bargains with other clever people, through friendships that are wholly transactional and dependent upon a quid pro quo, but that's simply the morality of an efficient insurance contract. I will help you because it is in my interest to do so, because I expect a return favor from you.[5] And that's the morality of pay-for-play, of K Street lobbyists, of the corrupt Clinton Cash Machine.

What empathy and the moral sense require is something other than the economist's rational calculation. As Blaise Pascal famously told us, "the heart has its reasons which reason knoweth not."[6] Morality is not a means of pursuing our rational self-interest, but an end in itself, proceeding from a good and not necessarily a clever heart, and the kindness I should have shown to my hydrocephalic classmate was its own reward, if any reward there was. The last chapter of Job, if canonical, might nevertheless be regretted.

The natural rights theorist will also struggle to explain empathy and fraternity. He would have you think that the opposite of natural law is anarchy and nihilism. It's not. It's revealed law, the law given to Moses and preached by Christ. Natural rights can tell you what others owe you, but not what you owe to others save for the thinnest of duties: don't harm them, don't steal from them or defraud them. Does that sound like a complete moral code? Does that tell me anything about my duties to my hydrocephalic classmate?

The revealed law's religious duties ask more of us, and have an emotional salience absent from abstract and rational explanations of behavior. "It makes some sense to speak of a loving God, a person," wrote Iris Murdoch, "but very little sense to speak of loving Good, a concept."[7] That was the meaning of Cardinal Newman's motto: *cor ad cor loquitur*, "heart speaks unto heart." It's why you can love your dog but not your goldfish. It's also why you can't love or even worship an impersonal god. You might as well worship Euclidian geometry. Only Blaise Pascal's God of Abraham, Isaac and Jacob, not of philosophers and scholars, can be loved.

And the emotional bond matters, when the religion's message is so pregnant with import, when it teaches us that we each have souls and each of us has an equal chance of meriting Heaven. That in turn means two things. First, aristocracy, family connections and the selfish gene are swept aside by Christ's terrible question, "Who is my mother and my brethren?" (Mark 3:33), which put paid to the family-based religions of the Ancient City's household gods.[8] Second, if I count no more than other people before God, then the words of the Declaration of Independence merely worked out ideas that were implicit in what Christ had taught. The eighteenth-century philosophes had plagiarized from an earlier text, for the individual and the ideal of equality had been invented many centuries before.[9]

All men are created equal. "Is that an empirical proposition?" Walter

Berns once asked me. If not, what is needed to believe it, other than religious belief? That is what I learned from the Sisters of Charity, that the lowest of lives is as precious as that of a clever economist. With their egalitarian principles, leftists claim to understand this better than the Right, and perhaps they do. What the Right had, in place of political egalitarianism, was religion. But what happens when the salt loses its savor, when religious lessons are no longer believed? What one is left with is what Tocqueville—himself a religious skeptic—called the hardest aristocracy that has appeared on earth.[10]

Before the advent of modern, secular liberalism, America's elite was Christian, in the high and dry manner of the Episcopalian businessman or the Unitarian lawyer. God had greatly provided for them, and they were wonderfully comfortable in Zion. Their religious observances were largely ceremonial, and they might have thought the religious enthusiast ridiculous, but some things were still forbidden to them. They were not permitted to mock the Irish serving girl or despise the Italian coal merchant. In their speeches, they would speak loftily of a common humanity, in the manner of Nelson Rockefeller. Since he was dyslexic, Rockefeller couldn't read his speeches, but he carried some 4 x 6 index cards and would refer to them. On one he wrote BOMFOG, and when he saw that card, he solemnly invoked the Brotherhood of Man and the Fatherhood of God.

When the religious imperative is stilled, however, the serving girl seems brassy and the coal merchant surly. They stand before us and impertinently demand our regard, ignoring our superiority, asserting a false equality, one no longer meaningful if God is dead. Nietzsche understood the Judeo-Christian basis for their insistence upon respect, and called this a "slave morality" and the product of *ressentiment*.[11] Call it resentment or call it religion, but the moral imperative remained so long as some semblance of religious belief remained. But when that was gone, the resentment was all in the other direction, by the Masters of the Universe against the polluting McDowell County coal miners, by the New Class against the deplorables, in the hardest aristocracy that has appeared on earth.

Modern liberalism is in crisis, having turned on itself and become illiberal. It has inherited a religious, Western culture in which it lives as an illegal alien, enjoying its harvest without planting the seed. A. J.

Balfour, the most intelligent of British prime ministers, predicted all of the twentieth century's atrocities when he saw where this would lead:

> Their spiritual life is parasitic: it is sheltered by convictions which belong, not to them, but to the society of which they form a part; it is nourished by processes in which they take no share. And when those convictions decay, and those processes come to an end, the alien life which they have maintained can scarce be expected to outlast them.[12]

Kant sought to prove the existence of God from the moral law.[13] He had it backwards. We more readily can infer the moral law from the existence of God. Without religious belief, everything is permitted, said Dostoyevsky; and equality is a tough sell. Among the wiser socialists, that realization has led to a new respect for religion as a foundation for their deepest beliefs. The religion that tells us "He hath put down the mighty from their seat, and hath exalted the humble" (Luke 1:52) must after all have some connection to equality. Without abandoning his atheism, therefore, the German philosopher Jürgen Habermas was willing to debate Cardinal Joseph Ratzinger (later Pope Benedict XVI) and announce his openness to learning from the egalitarian content of religious traditions.[14] So too, today's clever Marxist is more likely to read the Gospel according to St. Matthew than *Das Kapital*. But none of this would seem compelling to the secular members of the New Class, right and left, who have simply stopped caring about equality.

In 2016 modern liberalism died, exploded by its own illiberalism. This was the liberalism of scribes and Pharisees, of philosophes and savants, of columnists and comedians paid to spew venom. It was a liberalism that had lost its way and forgotten its religious origins, that smirked at believers, that preached equality without believing in it, that decried privilege while luxuriating in it. It was a liberalism without souls.

That's turned some conservatives into antiliberals. They've abandoned the liberal tradition of our Founders, forgetting how it was informed and shielded by religious belief, how the Judeo-Christian tradition teaches its own form of liberalism. The Sisters of Charity had never read John Locke, but with their faith, with their gentleness and sympathy for others, they had something better than a theory or a philosophy.

And Trump? Few people are less like the Curé d'Ars or Sister Simplice, but he nevertheless spoke with empathy about the Americans who had been left behind, and he did so without relying on abstract theories or invoking the spirit of geometry. He identified the hollowness of modern liberalism and appealed to a forgotten liberalism of compassion for fellow Americans. He cut through the bramble of failed intellectual doctrines to ask: How are you doing? Do you have a job? And having done so, he persuaded voters he could make things better. One saw all this in the enthusiasm of the crowds that turned up for his rallies, an enthusiasm that has not waned and which will likely propel him to victory in 2020.

CHAPTER 17

WHAT IS GREATNESS?

When Trump promised to "make America great again," when his supporters put on their red MAGA baseball caps, did they ever pause to wonder what makes a country great? Is it military greatness, perhaps? If so, they might have admired the world's great conquerors, such as Napoleon, and thrilled to the parade of military might on Red Square during the Soviet era. They would also have cheered the speech I heard Charles Krauthammer give at the American Enterprise banquet in 2014. After the fall of communism, said Krauthammer, American power reached to every corner of the world and exceeded that of any country in world history. There's glory for you, and greatness too!

Yet that wasn't what Trump supporters had in mind. The AEI banquet is called the "neocon prom," and if there's one thing Trump is not, it's a neocon. He went out of his way to denounce nation building in countries that were falling apart and promised to spend resources at home and not abroad. When he announced a modest troop buildup in Afghanistan, he said that the litmus test is our national interest. "We are not nation building again. We are killing terrorists."

There are other measures of greatness besides the military. Lorenzo the Magnificent's Florence had Michelangelo, Leonardo, Botticelli and Machiavelli. That's greatness, certainly. The London of Elizabeth I had Shakespeare, Marlowe, Spencer, Sydney, Jonson, Tallis and Byrd. The Paris of Louis XIV had Molière, Pascal, Corneille, Racine, Lully and Poussin. And us? We write the songs the whole world sings, but sometimes they're composed by Barry Manilow.

And yet we do have a time and a city that ranks with Florence, Paris and London, and that is late eighteenth-century Philadelphia, with George Washington, Thomas Jefferson, John Adams, Benjamin Franklin and Alexander Hamilton. "I think continually of those who were truly great," wrote Stephen Spender, and surely America's Founders are among those who left the vivid air signed with their honor.

If America is great, it's because of our Founders. If we once were great, and want to make America great again, it's their dream we need to recapture, a dream of equality and freedom memorably restated in the speeches of Abraham Lincoln. It's not about a military that can bomb any country back to the Stone Age. It's not about being the wealthiest country around, or else we might envy Norway's greatness. It's not even about a literary and musical heritage of which Americans are justly proud.

But while we might admire the ideals of the Founders, we can't go back to 1787. Nor would we want to. Even with their ideals, the Founders lived with too many things we would find unjust today. There were also injustices sixty years ago, but there was something special about the early 1960s. It was the last time that everyone thought we were great, that things would only get better, before it all went south. In 1962, *West Side Story* won Best Picture at the Academy Awards, and Edwin O'Connor's *The Edge of Sadness* won the Pulitzer Prize. The Beach Boys released "Surfin' Safari" and the New Lost City Ramblers sang "The Coo-Coo Bird." Martin Luther King led a desegregation march in Albany, Georgia, and James Meredith registered at the University of Mississippi. Pontiac introduced its 303 horsepower Grand Prix. Mickey Mantle's New York Yankees defeated Willie Mays's San Francisco Giants in the World Series, four games to three. John Glenn orbited the earth. John F. Kennedy said that a rising tide lifts all boats. Donald Trump was sixteen. If we wanted to make America great again, we'd want to feel about it today as we did then.

That was what Trump promised. That was what the MAGA slogan meant. It brought to mind something we had forgotten.

Here is what happened. A man had worn a jacket that he once had loved but which he feared might now seem dated. It was perfectly serviceable, and there was a time when its cut was the height of fashion, but more recently his new set of friends had scorned it. "How can you go on wearing that thing!" they told him. And so he cast it off.

Another man found it lying by the side of the road, picked it up and tried it on. It was wonderfully tailored, and while the fit was not quite perfect, it suited him well enough and he rolled up the sleeves and walked off with it.

The first man was a progressive. The coat was the liberalism of the old Democratic Party. The second man was Donald Trump.

The old coat, yesterday's liberalism, was dated but still handsome, and in many ways preferable to yesterday's conservatism. The coat was the party of John F. Kennedy, Arthur M. Schlesinger, Jr. and Lionel Trilling. They were authentic liberals who fought hard to expel the Communists from the Democratic Party. They believed that free markets made America great, and told us that lower taxes would get us moving again. On taxes and on racial matters, they were right and the conservatives of the day were wrong.

Today's Democrats belong to a very different party. With their race and gender triumphalism, with their identity politics, the progressives who dominate the party have abandoned Martin Luther King's vision of racially neutral laws and the idea that people should be judged according to the content of their character. Older liberals would be appalled by this, and by the progressives who shout down people with whom they disagree, who excuse Antifa thugs. Their party was an old coat they abandoned by the side of the road. It was left for Donald Trump to pick up the mantle of yesterday's Democrats.

The older Democrats believed in the American Dream, the idea that whoever you were, wherever you came from, this was the country where you could get ahead, and they'd be shocked to learn that we've become immobile, a class society in which the rich pass on their privileges to their children while the children of the poor inherit their parents' poverty. They'd be more shocked still if they learned that it was their party that was holding people back. Through broken K–12 schools, an idiotic immigration system, a broken rule of law, a regulatory state on steroids, all of which today's Democrats defend, we've placed a barrier in the path of Americans who seek to rise.

Yesterday's liberals were strong nationalists who knew that this was the greatest country on earth. They were patriots who loved America. They'd have had no use for people who see only its misdeeds, who take a knee when they hear the national anthem, who instinctively side with people who mock America. If we have our faults, as every country must, they knew that wouldn't stop us from meeting our challenges.

They stood up for what was right, they did splendid things, and their errors were mistakes of the mind and not the heart. By today's standards, they were economic liberals and social conservatives. They had an exhilarating confidence in our country's nobility and justice, and above all, in its greatness. We cannot recall them without yearning—*Dahin! dahin*—for the grandeur and innocence of that earlier time. Their passing left a hole in American politics, a hole that, with all his rudeness and bluster, with all the tweets and name-calling, Trump would fill. Henceforth, the future of American presidential politics is the Republican Workers Party.

*Tendebantque manus ripae ulterioris amore.**

Aeneid vi.314

---

* They were holding out their arms in longing for the farther shore.

APPENDICES

INCOME GROWTH IN THE UNITED STATES

	Pre-tax income growth 1946–80	Pre-tax income growth 1980–2014	Post-tax income growth 1946–80	Post-tax income growth 1980–2014
Full population	95%	61%	95%	61%
Bottom 50%	102%	1%	129%	21%
Top 10%	79%	121%	69%	113%
Top 1%	47%	204%	58%	194%
Top 0.01%	76%	453%	201%	423%

Source: Thomas Piketty, Emmanuel Saez and Gabriel Zucman, "Distributional National Accounts: Methods and Estimates for the United States," July 6, 2017, table 2.

APPENDIX 2

INTERGENERATIONAL IMMOBILITY

An immobility rating of zero indicates perfect mobility, with no correlation between the income bracket of parents and that of their children. A rating of 1.0 means there's absolute immobility, so that children always fall into the same income bracket as their parents. With a rating of 0.47, America is relatively immobile and nearly as aristocratic as Great Britain.

Country	Immobility
U.K.	0.50
Italy	0.48
U.S.	**0.47**
France	0.41
Spain	0.40
Germany	0.32
Sweden	0.27
Australia	0.26
Canada	0.19
Finland	0.18
Norway	0.17
Denmark	0.15

Source: Miles Corak, "Economic Mobility," *State of the Union: The Poverty and Inequality Report 2016*, Special Issue of *Pathway Magazine*, Stanford Center on Poverty and Inequality, 2016.

In Britain, with a rating of 0.5, a father earning £100,000 more than the average for his peers can expect that his son will earn £50,000 more than the average in his cohort. In more mobile Denmark, with a rating of 0.15, a father earning Kr100,000 more than his peers can expect that his son will end up closer to the mean, with a salary only Kr15,000 above the average. Canadian sons revert to the mean almost as quickly as Danish sons.

In the United States, as in Britain, the earnings advantage for a rich family will persist over several generations. If we start with a father whose salary is $400,000, which is $350,000 higher than the average, his son could be expected to earn $214,00 a year, his grandson $127,000 and his great-grandson $86,000. Bhashkar Mazumder suggests that the family might remain above average for longer than that. Using more sophisticated estimation techniques, he reports that the intergenerational mobility rating might be 0.6 and not 0.47, and even higher than 0.6 in top income brackets.* That rate might not seem so very high, but it amounts to roughly the same slow pace of regression to the mean that can be observed in the seedy great-grandchildren of nineteenth-century British grandees.

* Bhashkar Mazumder, "The Apple Falls Even Closer to the Tree Than We Thought: New and Revised Estimates of the Intergenerational Inheritance of Earnings," in *Unequal Chances: Family Background and Economic Success*, ed. Samuel Bowles, Herbert Gintis and Melissa O. Groves (Princeton, N.J.: Princeton University Press, 2005), 80; Bhashkar Mazumder, "Fortunate Sons: New Estimate of Intergenerational Mobility in the United States Using Social Security Earnings Data," *Review of Economics and Statistics* 87.2 (May 2005), 235–55.

APPENDIX 3

INTERGENERATIONAL MOBILITY IN THE UNITED STATES AND CANADA

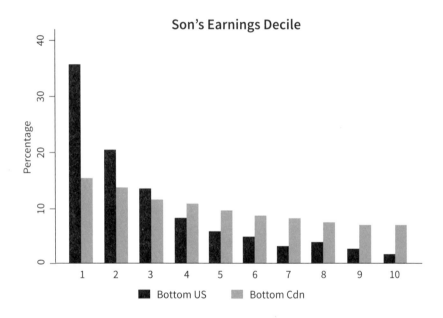

Son's Earnings Decile

Earnings Deciles of Sons Born to Bottom-Decile Fathers, U.S. and Canada

The horizontal axis shows the income deciles of sons born to bottom-decile fathers: lowest decile on the left, highest on the right. The vertical axis indicates the percentage of sons who end up in each decile. Among American sons of fathers in the bottom 10 percent in earnings, around 37 percent will end up in the bottom decile themselves, while for Canadian sons of bottom 10 percent fathers the proportion is only about 16 percent.

Conversely, a bottom 10 percent father in Canada is much more likely to have a son in the top 10 percent than is a bottom-decile American father.

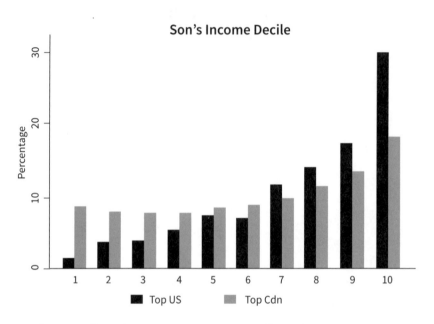

Earnings Deciles of Sons Born to Top-Decile Fathers, U.S. and Canada

Among the sons of top-decile American fathers, nearly 30 percent will end up in the top decile themselves, versus about 18 percent in Canada. Few sons of American top 10 percent fathers will descend to the bottom of the ladder, while a substantial proportion of the Canadian sons will do so.

Sources: Miles Corak, Lori J. Curtis and Shelly Phipps, "Economic Mobility, Family Background, and Well-Being of Children in the United States and Canada," in *Persistence, Privilege, and Parenting: The Comparative Study of Intergenerational Mobility*, ed. Timothy M. Smeeding, Robert Erikson and Markus Jäntti (New York: Russell Sage, 2011), 73, 76–78; Tom Hertz, "Rags, Riches, and Race: The Intergenerational Mobility of Black and White Families in the United States," in *Unequal Chances: Family Background and Economic Success*, ed. Samuel Bowles, Herbert Gintis and Melissa O. Groves (Princeton, N.J.: Princeton University Press, 2005), 165, table 5.10.

APPENDIX 4

PISA STUDENT PERFORMANCE SCORES, 2015

	Rank (math)	Math	Science	Reading	Spending per upper secondary student (PPP)
Singapore	1	564	556	535	n/a
Japan	2	532	538	516	n/a
Switzerland	8	521	506	592	16,521
Canada	**9**	**516**	**528**	**527**	**11,607**
Netherlands	10	512	509	503	12,171
Finland	13	511	531	526	8,467
Denmark	14	511	502	500	10,908
Germany	16	506	509	509	12,022
Ireland	18	504	503	521	11,576
Poland	18	504	501	506	5,764
Norway	19	502	513	503	14,838
New Zealand	22	495	513	509	10,023
Australia	25	494	510	503	9,859
U.K.	29	492	509	498	6,491
U.S.	**38**	**470**	**496**	**497**	**13,143**
OECD Average		490	493	493	9,506

Sources: OECD, "Snapshot of performance in science, reading and mathematics," *PISA 2015 Results in Focus* (2018), 5; OECD, "How much is spent per student?" *Education at a Glance 2014: OECD Indicators* (2014), 204, Indicator B1.

ACKNOWLEDGMENTS

I give thanks to the many people who've helped me, to Howard Anglin, Michael Anton, Larry Arnn, David Azerrad, Ken Bauerlein, Darren Beattie, Dan Bonevac, Nick Capaldi, Chris Buskirk, Angelo Codevilla, Lionel Chetwynd, Mark Cunningham, David DesRosiers, Allen Guelzo, Alex Hoyt, Doug Jeffrey, Robert Jeffrey, Rob Koons, Tom Lindsay, Ron Maxwell, Dan McCarthy, Jim Piereson, Stephen Presser, Al Regnery, Richard Reinsch, Rusty Reno, John Samples, Roger Simon, Matthew Spaulding, James Taranto, Peter Thiel, Ben Weingarten and my old friend Bob Tyrrell. Sadly, Ron Rotunda, whose comments were always most helpful, passed away in March 2018.

My research assistant, Bob Minchin (Scalia Law 2020), was of enormous help. You'd do well to hire him.

I received very useful comments when presenting my ideas at the Cato Institute, Florida Southern College, the Fund for American Studies, Hillsdale College, James Madison College, the John Locke Foundation, the Manning Center, the McDonald-Laurier Institute, Saint Vincent College, the University of Detroit Law School, the University of Wisconsin Law School, the Women of Washington and Washington and Lee Law School.

Portions of this book were taken from my writings at the *American Conservative*, the *American Spectator*, Fox News, the *New York Post*, Real Clear Politics, the *Wall Street Journal* and the *UCLA Law Review*.

I also thank George Mason's Scalia Law School for its generous support. Esther Koblenz at the Scalia law library and Susan Birchler were extremely helpful.

My heartfelt thanks to everyone at Encounter Books, to the production team of Heather Ohle and Katherine Wong and the marketing team of Sam Schneider and Lauren Miklos, to Carol Staswick for her superb editing and especially to Roger Kimball.

This book would not have been possible without the encouragement and invaluable organizational and editorial assistance offered by my wife, Esther Goldberg, whose help I cannot adequately acknowledge.

F.H. Buckley
Alexandria, Virginia
April 10, 2018

NOTES

CHAPTER 1. HOW THE HELL DID WE GET HERE?

1 Christine Lagarde, "The Challenge Facing the Global Economy: New Momentum to Overcome a New Mediocre," International Monetary Fund, October 2, 2014.

2 Christopher Lasch, *The Revolt of the Elites and the Betrayal of Democracy* (New York: W. W. Norton, 1995); Milovan Djilas, *The New Class: An Analysis of the Communist System* (New York: Praeger, 1957).

3 Max Horkheimer and Theodor W. Adorno, *Dialectic of Enlightenment*, ed. Gunzelin Schmid Noerr, trans. Edmund Jephcott (1947; Palo Alto, Calif.: Stanford University Press, 2002), 21. See also Georg Lukács, *History and Class Consciousness: Studies in Marxist Dialectics*, trans. Rodney Livingston (Cambridge, Mass.: MIT Press, 1971), 48.

CHAPTER 2. A TIME FOR CHOOSING

1 Peter Schweizer, *Clinton Cash: The Untold Story of How and Why Foreign Governments and Businesses Helped Make Bill and Hillary Rich* (New York: Harper, 2015).

2 Editorial, "Cutting Ties to the Clinton Foundation," *New York Times*, August 30, 2016.

3 Isabel Vincent, "Charity Watchdog: Clinton Foundation a 'Slush Fund,'" *New York Post*, April 26, 2015.

4 Erik Wasson, "Obama: Not 'Even a Smidgen of Corruption' behind Internal Revenue Service Targeting," *The Hill*, February 2, 2014.

5 Editorial, "The Real Internal Revenue Scandal," *New York Times*, July 5, 2014.

6 Lauren French, "Two Democrats Call for Ethics Probe into J. Russell George's Work as IRS Inspector General," *Politico*, February 7, 2014.

7 Hillary Clinton, *What Happened* (New York: Simon & Schuster, 2017). Mrs. Clinton followed up the book with interviews in the same vein.

8 Michael Kelly, "Saint Hillary," *New York Times Magazine*, May 23, 1993.

9 Charles Baudelaire, *Œuvres complètes*, vol. 1 (Paris: Gallimard, 1975), 693.

10 F.H. Buckley, *The Once and Future King* (New York: Encounter Books, 2014).

11 Blaise Pascal, *Œuvres complètes*, vol. 2 (Paris: Gallimard, 2000), 677 (§ 397).

12 Michael Tanner, "The American Welfare State: How We Spend Nearly $1 Trillion a Year Fighting Poverty—and Fail," Cato Institute, Policy Analysis no. 694 (April 11, 2012).

13 Derrick Morgan, "Reform the Welfare State, Don't Enlarge It with Amnesty," Heritage Foundation, July 3, 2013.

14 Willem Adema, Pauline Fron and Maxime Ladaique, "Is the European Welfare State Really More Expensive? Indicators on Social Spending 1980–2012," OECD Social, Employment and Migration Working Paper no. 124 (November, 2, 2011), 33, table I.4, and 34, chart I.11.

15 David Hume, "Idea of a Perfect Commonwealth," in *Hume: Political Essays* (New York: Cambridge University Press, 1994), 222.

16 Henry Adams, "The Education of Henry Adams," in *Adams: Democracy, Esther, Mont Saint Michel and Chartres, The Education of Henry Adams* (New York: Library of America, 1983), 1101.

17 Joshua Green, "How to Get Trump Elected When He's Wrecking Everything You Built," *Bloomberg Businessweek*, May 26, 2016.

18 F.H. Buckley, *The Way Back: Restoring the Promise of America* (New York: Encounter Books, 2016).

CHAPTER 3. THE CAMPAIGN TAKES SHAPE

1 At the time, none of us knew about how the Russians sought to influence the election, and even now we seem to know little of the story. We've not seen evidence that the Trump campaign colluded with the Russians, but we do know that the Democratic Party through intermediaries paid for Russian dirt against Trump. We've also conveniently forgotten how Obama's Democrats sought to influence an Israeli election, and how NGOs we had financed supported Putin's opponents in Russia. If they were messing with us, we had first messed with them. In any event, a reset of relations with Russia remains a worthy goal if this might reverse its brutal disregard of international norms.

2 F.H. Buckley, "Trump vs. the New Class," *American Conservative*, May 2, 2016.

3 Derek Thompson, "Is $250,000 a Year Really 'Middle Income'?" *Atlantic*, September 14, 2012.

4 Dan Balz, *Collision 2012: Obama vs. Romney and the Future of Elections in America* (New York: Viking, 2013), chap. 23.

5 Suzanne Mettler, *The Submerged State: How Invisible Government Policies Undermine American Democracy* (Chicago: University of Chicago Press, 2011).

CHAPTER 4. MEETINGS WITH REMARKABLE PEOPLE

1 Nicholas Antongiavanni, *The Suit: A Machiavellian Approach to Men's Style* (New York: Collins, 2006).

2 Michael T. Flynn, "Our ally Turkey is in crisis and needs our support," *The Hill*, November 8, 2016. See Dion Nissenbaum, "Flynn's Pro-Turkey Work: Unfinished Film," *Wall Street Journal*, May 31, 2017.

CHAPTER 5. DECLINE

1 Whittaker Chambers, *Witness* (1952; South Bend, Ind.: Regnery, 1979), 196.

2 Caddell & Associates, Survey of US Voters, March 10, 2016.

3 Thomas Piketty, *Capital in the Twenty-First Century* (Cambridge, Mass.: Harvard University Press, 2013), 87.

4 Nicholas Eberstadt, "Our Miserable 21st Century," *Commentary*, February 15, 2017.

5 That's the aggregate economy. It's not GDP per capita. The U.S. population has increased by about 1 percent a year (about twice as much as that of China). If we had experienced 1 percent growth in both aggregate GDP and the size of our population, there would be no change in GDP per capita over the hundred-year period. As for what's ahead, the technology skeptic Robert Gordon argues that the pace of innovation has stalled and forecasts average growth in real per capita income of only 0.7 per year over the next quarter century. Robert J. Gordon, *The Rise and Fall of American Growth: The U.S. Standard of Living Since the Civil War* (Princeton, N.J.: Princeton University Press, 2016).

6 Robert Cooter and Aaron Edlin, "Overtaking," in *The American Illness: Essays in the Rule of Law*, ed. F.H. Buckley (New Haven: Yale University Press, 2013).

CHAPTER 6. WHERE DID THE DREAM GO?

1 Karl Marx, *The Eighteenth Brumaire of Louis Napoleon*, trans. Daniel DeLeon, 3rd ed. (Chicago: Charles H. Kerr, 1913), 21–22.

2 Seymour Martin Lipset and Gary Wolfe Marks, *It Didn't Happen Here: Why Socialism Failed in the United States* (New York: W. W. Norton, 2001).

3 See Appendix B in F.H. Buckley, *The Way Back: Restoring the Promise of America* (New York: Encounter Books, 2016), 291.

4 Congressional Budget Office, "Trends in Family Wealth, 1989 to 2013," August 2016.

5 Mark R. Rank, "From Rags to Riches to Rags," *New York Times Magazine*, April 18, 2014.

6 Scott Winship, "The Great Gatsby Curve: All Heat, No Light," Brookings Institution, May 20, 1985.

7 Raj Chetty et al., "The Fading American Dream: Trends in Absolute Income Mobility since 1940," NBER Working Paper no. 22910, National Bureau of Economic Research (December 2016).

8 Raj Chetty et al., "Where Is the Land of Opportunity? The Geography of Intergenerational Mobility in the United States," NBER Working Paper no. 19843, National Bureau of Economic Research (January 2014).

9 Richard Dawkins, *The Selfish Gene* (Oxford, UK: Oxford University Press, 2006). W. D. Hamilton's breakthrough articles on inclusive fitness may be found in his collected essays, *Narrow Roads of Gene Land*, vol. 1, *Evolution of Social Behaviour* (Oxford, UK: W. H. Freeman, 1996), chap. 2, "Hamilton's Rule."

CHAPTER 7. TWO-DIMENSIONAL MAN

1 Herbert Marcuse, *One-Dimensional Man: Studies in the Ideology of Advanced Industrial Society* (Boston: Beacon Press, 1964).

2 On being confronted with Drutman's findings, some libertarians suggested that the table be reconfigured with a new center of gravity at the weighted center of the distribution, to the left of the 0, 0 axis. But that would simply make people with left-wing economic views look like libertarians.

3 Herbert Butterfield, *The Whig Interpretation of History* (New York: W. W. Norton, 1965).

4 Sarah Pulliam Bailey, "Could religious institutions lose tax-exempt status over Supreme Court's gay marriage case?" *Washington Post*, April 28, 2015.

5 Michael McGough, "Feinstein, a Catholic nominee and a dogma that didn't bark," *Los Angeles Times*, September 8, 2017.

6 Marc Thiessen, "Hillary Clinton's War of Faith," *New York Post*, October 15, 2016.

7 Terry Eagleton, *Culture and the Death of God* (New Haven: Yale University Press, 2015), 20–26.

8 Carl L. Becker, *The Heavenly City of the Eighteenth-Century Philosophers*, 2nd ed. (New Haven: Yale University Press, 2003), 31.

9 *Obergefell v. Hodges*, 576 U.S. _____ (2015).

10 In re Sweetcakes, Bureau of Labor and Industries, no. 44-15 & 45-15 (July 2, 2015). On narrow grounds, the Supreme Court recently upheld the religious rights of a baker to refuse to create a wedding cake for a same-sex couple. *Masterpiece Cakeshop, Ltd. v. Colorado Civil Rights Commission*, _ U.S. _ (2018). A member of the Colorado commission had described the baker's assertion of his religious rights as "one of the most despicable pieces of rhetoric that people can use," and likened it to the Holocaust. Civil rights commissioners will learn how to hide their hostility to religion in future cases.

11 Claire Foran, "Is There Any Room in the 'Big Tent' for Pro-Life Democrats?" *Atlantic*, April 27, 2017.

CHAPTER 8. NATIONALISM

1 See Stephen Kantrowitz, *Ben Tillman and the Reconstruction of White Supremacy* (Chapel Hill: University of North Carolina Press, 2000).

2 Henry St. John, Viscount Bolingbroke, *The Idea of a Patriot King* (1738), in *Political Writings*, ed. David Armitage (New York: Cambridge University Press, 1997), 257–58.

3 *Shropshire Conservative*, August 31, 1844, quoted in William Flavelle Monypenny, *The Life of Benjamin Disraeli*, vol. 2 (New York: Macmillan, 1917), 231.

4 Benjamin Disraeli, Speech at Edinburgh on Reform Bill, October 1867, in *Selected Speeches of the Late and Right Honourable Earl of Beaconsfield*, ed. T. E. Kebbel (London: Longmans, Green, 1882), vol. 2:488.

5 On Tory Democracy, see R. F. Foster, *Lord Randolph Churchill: A Political Life* (Oxford, UK: Oxford University Press, 1981); R. E. Quinault, "Lord Randolph Churchill and Tory Democracy, 1880–1885," *Historical Journal* 22.1 (March 1979), 141–65. On Canadian Toryism, see the two-volume biography of John Macdonald by Donald Creighton, *The Young Politician* and *The Old Chieftain* (Toronto: Macmillan, 1952 & 1955); and George Grant, *Lament for a Nation: The Defeat of Canadian Nationalism* (Ottawa: Carleton Library Series, 2005).

6 Peter Beinart, "The Racial and Religious Paranoia of Trump's Warsaw Speech," *Atlantic*, July 6, 2017.

7 Rémi Brague, *Eccentric Culture: A Theory of Western Civilization* (South Bend, Ind.: St. Augustine's Press, 2002).

8 Abraham Lincoln, Speech at Chicago, Illinois, July 10, 1858, in *Lincoln: Speeches and Writings 1832–1858* (New York: Library of America, 1989), 456.

9 Pauline Maier, *American Scripture: Making the Declaration of Independence* (New York: Vintage, 1997). See also Michael Kammen, *A Machine That Would Go of Itself: The Constitution in American Culture* (New York: St. Martin's, 1994); Yael Tamir, *Liberal Nationalism* (Princeton, N.J.: Princeton University Press, 1993).

10 *Texas v. Johnson*, 491 U.S. 397 (1989).

11 Simone Weil, *L'Enracinement, prélude à une déclaration des devoirs envers l'être humain* (Paris: Gallimard, 1949); translated (by Arthur Wills) as *The Need for Roots: Prelude to a Declaration of Duties toward Mankind* (London: Routledge, 1952).

12 Miller McPherson, Lynn Smith-Lovin and Matthew E. Brashears, "Social Isolation in America: Changes in Core Discussion Networks over Two Decades," *American Sociological Review* 71.3 (June 2006), 353–75.

CHAPTER 9. HOW TO BRING BACK OUR MOJO

1 Ludger Woessmann et al., "School Accountability, Autonomy, Choice, and the Level of Student Achievement: International Evidence from PISA 2003," OECD Education Working Paper no. 13 (OECD Publishing, November 14, 2008), 20.

2 Eric A. Hanushek, Paul E. Peterson and Ludger Woessmann, *Endangering Prosperity: A Global View of the American School* (Washington, D.C.: Brookings Institution Press, 2013), 12, 61–63.

3 That is, when the dollars are equalized according to the ability to purchase a basket of basic goods on local markets. See Eric A. Hanushek and Alfred A. Lindseth, *Schoolhouses, Courthouses, and Statehouses: Solving the Funding-Achievement Puzzle in America's Public Schools* (Princeton, N.J.: Princeton University Press, 2009).

4 Ibid., 40–42.

5 Aria Bendix, "Do Private-School Vouchers Promote Segregation?" *Atlantic*, May 22, 2017.

6 Rebecca Mead, "Betsy DeVos and the Plan to Break Public Schools," *New Yorker*, December 14, 2016.

7 Valerie Strauss, "Some Kindergartners to Learn about Gender Identity amid Push for New Health Education Standards," *Washington Post*, July 8, 2016.

8 Debbie Truong, "School Boards Increasingly Embrace the ABCs of Social Activism," *Washington Post*, February 17, 2018.

9 *Zelman v. Simmons-Harris*, 536 U.S. 639 (2002).

10 See *Mitchell v. Helms*, 530 U.S. 793, 828–29 (plurality opinion of Thomas, J., joined by Rehnquist, C.J., and Scalia and Kennedy, JJ.) (2000).

11 Philip Hamburger, *Separation of Church and State* (Cambridge, Mass.: Harvard University Press, 2002).

12 It's upper-class voters who most object to school choice. See, e.g., John J. Miller, "Why School Choice Lost," *Wall Street Journal*, November 3, 1993.

13 David Lauter, "Education: Trump Wants More Money for Vouchers, Cuts Elsewhere," *Los Angeles Times*, March 16, 2017.

14 George J. Borjas, *Immigration Economics* (Cambridge, Mass.: Harvard University Press, 2014), 152–53.

15 George J. Borjas, "Making It in America: Social Mobility in the Immigrant Population," *Future of Children* 16.2 (Fall 2006), 55–71.

16 Borjas, *Immigration Economics*, 94. See also George J. Borjas, *We Wanted Workers: Unraveling the Immigration Narrative* (New York: W. W. Norton, 2016); Patricia Cortes, "The Effect of Low-Skilled Immigration on U.S. Prices: Evidence from CPI Data," *Journal of Political Economy* 116.3 (June 2008), 381–422 (finding a 2 percent drop in low-skilled wages on a 10 percent increase in immigration levels). For a summary of the debate concluding that immigration takes jobs from some Americans but on average is neutral, see National Academies of Sciences, Engineering, and Medicine, *The Economic and Fiscal Consequences of Immigration* (Washington, D.C.: National Academies Press, 2016).

17 George J. Borjas, Jeffrey Grogger and Gordon H. Hanson, "Immigration and the Economic Status of African-American Men," *Economica* 77.306 (April 2010), 255–82 (using 1960–2000 data).

18 See, e.g., George J. Borjas, *Heaven's Door: Immigration Policy and the American Economy* (Princeton, N.J.: Princeton University Press, 1999), 192–93. Two years ago the Trump campaign knew that there would be a call to admit the "Dreamers" whom Obama purported to legalize under the DACA program, and that this should be done as part of a broad immigration package that included replacing the 1965 Immigration Act with the Canadian points system. Americans are dreamers too.

19 David A. Green and Christopher Worswick, "Entry Earnings of Immigrant Men in Canada: The Roles of Labour Market Entry Effects and Returns to Foreign Experience," in *Canadian Immigration: Economic Evidence for a Dynamic Policy Environment*, ed. Ted McDonald et al. (Kingston, Ont.: McGill-Queen's University Press, 2010), 77–110.

20 Sean Coughlan, "How Canada Became an Education Superpower," BBC News, August 2, 2017.

21 Alan J. Auerbach and Philip Oreopoulos, "The Fiscal Effect of U.S. Immigration: A Generational-Accounting Perspective," *Tax Policy and the Economy* 14 (2000), 123–56; Michael J. Greenwood and John M. McDowell, *Legal U.S. Immigration: Influences on Gender, Age, and Skill Composition* (Kalamazoo: W. E. Upjohn, 1999).

22 Abdurrhaman Aydemir, Wen-Hao Chen and Miles Corak, "Intergenerational Earnings Mobility among the Children of Canadian Immigrants," IZA Discussion Paper no. 2085 (April 2006).

23 Statistics Canada, *Immigration and Ethnocultural Diversity in Canada: National Household Survey 2011* (Ottawa, 2013).

24 In addition, some of the illegals performed tasks that freed up Americans to work more productively, and some created new jobs for Americans. The illegals had to buy food and clothing, usually from American sellers.

25 Lisa M. Krieger, "Can a Pay Raise Fix Agriculture Industry's Labor Crisis in California? Yes and No," *Washington Post*, July 30, 2017.

26 World Bank, *Where Is the Wealth of Nations? Measuring Capital for the 21st Century* (Washington, D.C., 2006). On the positive relation between economic growth and the rule of law, see Robert J. Barro and Xavier Sala-i-Martin, *Economic Growth*, 2nd ed. (Cambridge, Mass.: MIT Press, 2004), 526–29; Daron Acemoglu, *Introduction to Modern Economic Growth* (Princeton, N.J.: Princeton University Press, 2009), 123–40.

27 José Ortega y Gasset, *The Revolt of the Masses* (New York: W. W. Norton, 1932), 12.

28 Mancur Olson, *The Rise and Decline of Nations: Economic Growth, Stagflation, and Social Rigidities* (New Haven: Yale University Press, 1982).

CHAPTER 10. WHAT IS A JOBS PRESIDENT?

1 These numbers might need some adjusting, lest we compare American apples to Canadian oranges. The unemployment rate is higher in Canada, but then there are more Americans in the military or in prison.

2 Congressional Budget Office, International Comparison of Corporate Income Tax Rates, March 2017.

3 David Wessel, "Big U.S. Firms Shift Hiring Abroad," *Wall Street Journal*, April 19, 2011.

4 Tyler Cowen, *The Complacent Class: The Self-Defeating Quest for the American Dream* (New York: St. Martin's, 2017).

5 Raven Molloy, Christopher L. Smith and Abigail Wozniak, "Declining Migration Within the US: The Role of the Labor Market," Federal Reserve Board, April 2014.

6 Claudia Goldin and Lawrence F. Katz, *The Race between Education and Technology* (Cambridge, Mass.: Harvard University Press, 2008); R. Jason Faberman and Bhashkar Mazumder, "Is there a skills mismatch in the labor market?" *Chicago Fed Letter*, July 2012.

7 Donald Trump, Remarks at the White House, March 17, 2017.

8 See David Leonhardt, "The Trouble with Trade School," *New York Times*, July 17, 2017.

9 Alan B. Krueger, "Where Have All the Workers Gone?" Federal Reserve Bank of Boston, October 4, 2016.

10 National Institute on Drug Abuse, "Opioid Overdose Crisis," June 2017 (rev. March 2018); Beth Han et al., "Prescription Opioid Use, Misuse, and Use Disorders in U.S. Adults: 2015 National Survey on Drug Use and Health," *Annals of Internal Medicine*, August 1, 2017.

11 David H. Autor and Mark G. Duggan, "The Growth in the Social Security Disability Insurance Rolls: A Fiscal Crisis Unfolding," *Journal of Economic Perspectives* 20.3 (Summer 2006), 71–96.

12 The proportion of those not in the labor force who received disability benefits rose from 38.3 percent in 1985 to 56.5 percent in 2013. Nicholas Eberstadt, *Men Without Work: America's Invisible Crisis* (West Conshohocken, Penn.: Templeton Press, 2016), 118–19.

13 Malcolm S. Salter, "Crony Capitalism American Style: What Are We Talking About Here?" Harvard Business School Working Paper no. 15-025 (October 22, 2014). See Timothy P. Carney, *The Big Ripoff: How Big Business and Big Government Steal Your Money* (Hoboken, N.J.: John Wiley, 2006).

CHAPTER 11. DRAINING THE SWAMP

1 Niall Stanage, "Is Trump a Victim of the 'Deep State'?" *The Hill*, June 5, 2017.

2 Greg Miller, "At CIA, a watchful eye on Mike Pompeo, the president's ardent ally," *Washington Post*, August 25, 2017.

3 Michael J. Glennon, *National Security and Double Government* (Oxford, UK: Oxford University Press, 2014).

4 *Texas v. U.S.*, 579 U.S. _____ (2016).

5 Bentley Coffey, Patrick A. McLaughlin and Pietro Peretto, "The Cumulative Cost of Regulations," Mercatus Working Paper, April 2016.

6 Edward Gibbon, *The Decline and Fall of the Roman Empire* (New York: Knopf, 1994), vol. 4:419.

7 Edwin A. Miles, "The First People's Inaugural—1829," *Tennessee Historical Quarterly* 37.3 (Fall 1978), 293–307.

8 Ari Hoogenboom, "The Pendleton Act and the Civil Service," *American Historical Review* 64.2 (January 1959), 301–18.

9 Max Weber, "Technical Advantages of Bureaucratic Organization," in *From Max Weber: Essays in Sociology*, ed. Hans Heinrich Gerth and C. Wright Mills (London: Routledge & Kegan Paul, 1970), 215.

10 William A. Niskanen, *Bureaucracy and Representative Government* (Piscataway, N.J.: Transaction, 1971).

11 Juliet Eilperin, Lisa Rein and Marc Fisher, "Resistance from within: Federal workers push back against Trump," *Washington Post*, January 31, 2017.

12 Jonathan Swan, "Government workers shun Trump, give big money to Clinton," *The Hill*, October 26, 2016.

13 Lord Hewart, *The New Despotism* (London: Ernest Benn, 1929).

14 Philip Hamburger, *Is Administrative Law Unlawful?* (Chicago: University of Chicago Press, 2014).

15 Arthur M. Schlesinger, Jr., *The Age of Jackson* (Boston: Little, Brown, 1945), 46–47.

16 F.H. Buckley, *The Republic of Virtue: How We Tried to Ban Corruption, Failed, and What We Can Do about It* (New York: Encounter Books, 2017).

17 Pub. L. 110-81, 121 Stat. 735. 2 U.S.C. § 1613.

18 Thomas B. Edsall, "The Trouble with That Revolving Door," *New York Times*, December 18, 2011.

19 Quoted in Lawrence Lessig, *Republic, Lost: How Money Corrupts Congress—and a Plan to Stop It* (New York: Twelve, 2011), 123.

20 Brice McKeever, "The Nonprofit Sector in Brief 2015: Public Charities, Giving, and Volunteering," Urban Institute, October 29, 2015.

21 I am indebted to Jim Piereson for this suggestion. "Private foundations" should be defined to exclude churches, colleges and hospitals, and to include only the foundations referred to in 26 USC § 509(a)(2).

22 F.H. Buckley, *The Way Back: Restoring the Promise of America* (New York: Encounter Books, 2016), 212–14.

23 11 U.S.C. § 523(a)(8), P. Law 95-598, 92 Stat. § 2591.

24 Danny Vinik, "Inside the new battle against Google," *Politico*, September 17, 2017. See also Craig Timberg, "Could Google Rankings Skew an Election? New Group Aims to Find Out," *Washington Post*, March 14, 2007.

25 Brody Mullins and Jack Nicas, "Paying Professors: Inside Google's Academic Influence Campaign," *Wall Street Journal*, July 14, 2017.

26 Lina M. Khan, "Amazon's Antitrust Paradox," *Yale Law Journal* 126.3 (January 2017), 710.

27 Luther Lowe, "It's Time to Bust the Online Trusts," *Wall Street Journal*, November 1, 2017; Jonathan Taplin, *Move Fast and Break Things: How Facebook, Google and Amazon Cornered Culture and Undermined Democracy* (New York: Little, Brown, 2017).

28 Thomas J. DiLorenzo, "The Myth of Natural Monopoly," *Review of Austrian Economics* 9.2 (1996), 43–58.

29 Microsoft's Bill Gates was a "rich spoiled brat," warned Maureen Dowd, and Microsoft was an "egomaniacal, dangerous giant that has cut off the air supply of competitors in a bid to control cyberspace." Maureen Dowd, "Liberties; Revenge on the Nerds," *New York Times*, January 21, 1998.

30 Senate Bill 1424, California Legislature, 2017–2018 Regular Session (March 22, 2018).

CHAPTER 12. HOW THE CONSTITUTION CREATED THE REPUBLICAN WORKERS PARTY

1 Roger Shattuck, *Forbidden Knowledge: From Prometheus to Pornography* (New York: Mariner Books, 1997).

2 F.H. Buckley, *The Once and Future King: The Rise of Crown Government in America* (New York: Encounter Books, 2014).

3 David R. Mayhew, *Divided We Govern: Party Control, Lawmaking, and Investigations, 1946–2002* (New Haven: Yale University Press, 2005), 76.

CHAPTER 13. WHICH SIDE ARE YOU ON?

1 Wesley Lowery, "All-you-can-brawl in small-town West Virginia," *Washington Post*, March 29, 2017.

2 Michael Weisskopf, "Energized by Pulpit or Passion, the Public Is Calling," *Washington Post*, February 1, 1993.

3 Ed Pilkington, "Obama Angers Midwest Voters with Guns and Religion Remark," *Guardian*, April 14, 2008.

4 David Brooks, "How We Are Ruining America," *New York Times,* July 11, 2017.

5 Jonah Goldberg, "'New Nationalism' Amounts to Generic White Identity Politics," *National Review*, August 17, 2016.

6 Madison Park, "Ben Shapiro Spoke at Berkeley as Protesters Gathered Outside," CNN, September 15, 2017.

7 See, e.g., Margaret Sullivan, "Quick to vilify antifa, but slow to explain it," *Washington Post*, September 4, 2017; Carlos Lozada, "How antifa justifies stifling speech, clobbering supremacists," *Washington Post*, September 3, 2017; Mark Bray, "What the 'alt-left' antifa activists actually believe," *Washington Post*, August 20, 2017; Perry Stein, "What draws Americans to anarchy? It's more than just smashing windows," *Washington Post*, August 10, 2017, quoting a young anarchist: "'It takes awhile to get used to the label [of anarchist] because it comes with a lot of baggage,' LeMaster said. 'People assume that anarchism is so extreme. But I associate it with wanting everyone's needs to be met.'"

8 Scholars and Writers for America, https://scholarsandwritersforamerica.org/.

9 Daniel Strauss, "Clinton Haunted by Coal Country Comment," *Politico*, May 10, 2016.

10 James Agee and Walker Evans, *Let Us Now Praise Famous Men: Three Tenant Families*, in *Agee: Let Us Now Praise Famous Men, A Death in the Family, and Shorter Fiction*, ed. Michael Sragow (New York: Library of America, 2005), 23.

11 Michael Harrington, *The Other America: Poverty in the United States* (New York: Scribner, 1962).

12 Maurice Isserman, *The Other American: The Life of Michael Harrington* (New York: PublicAffairs, 2000), 70–84.

13 Thomas Frank, *Listen, Liberal: Whatever Happened to the Party of the People?* (New York: Henry Holt, 2016).

14 Benjamin Disraeli, *Sybil, or the Two Nations* (London: Longmans, Green, 1871), 76–77.

15 Mark Muro and Sifan Liu, "Another Clinton-Trump divide: High-output America vs Low-output America," Brookings Institution, November 29, 2016.

16 Robert A. Dahl, *Democracy in the United States: Promise and Performance* (Chicago: Rand McNally, 1972), 309.

17 Caitlin Flanagan, "How Late-Night Comedy Fueled the Rise of Trump," *Atlantic*, May 2017.

18 Editorial, *Washington Post*, February 29, 2016.

CHAPTER 14. THE PLEA OF IMPOSSIBILITY

1 Arthur O. Lovejoy, *The Great Chain of Being: A Study in the History of an Idea* (Cambridge, Mass.: Harvard University Press, 1936).

2 See, e.g., David H. Autor, Lawrence F. Katz and Melissa S. Kearney, "Trends in U.S. Wage Inequality: Revising the Revisionists," *Review of Economics and Statistics* 90.2 (May 2008), 300–23; Daron Acemoglu, "Technical Change, Inequality, and the Labor Market," *Journal of Economic Literature* 40.1 (March 2002), 7–72.

3 Ian D. Wyatt and Daniel E. Hecker, "Occupational Changes during the 20th Century," *Monthly Labor Review* 29.3 (March 2006), 54, chart 17, and 55.

CHAPTER 15. THE ANATOMY OF INDIFFERENCE

1 Simon Baron-Cohen, *The Science of Evil: On Empathy and the Origins of Cruelty* (New York: Basic Books, 2011).

2 Carol Gilligan, *In a Different Voice: Psychological Theory and Women's Development* (Harvard University Press, 1982). Gilligan's book, hugely influential when it first appeared, sits less well today with those who believe that gender differences are entirely culture-driven. Thinking otherwise can get you fired at Google.

3 Grant Gilmore, *The Ages of American Law* (New Haven: Yale University Press, 1977), 111.

4 Lawrence Kohlberg, *Essays on Moral Development: The Philosophy of Moral Development* (San Francisco: Harper & Row, 1981), 12–13.

5 Whittaker Chambers, *Witness* (1952; Washington, D.C.: Regnery Gateway, 1980), 133–37; Victor Hugo, *Les misérables* (Paris: Gallimard, 1951), 313.

6 Robert Cooter and Peter Rappoport, "Were the Ordinalists Wrong about Welfare Economics?" *Journal of Economic Literature* 22.2 (June 1984), 507–30.

7 See Bertrand de Jouvenel, *The Ethics of Redistribution* (Indianapolis: Liberty Fund, 1990). The supple Jouvenel was a fascist *avant-guerre* and a libertarian *après-guerre*.

8 Philanthropy Roundtable, "Who Gives Most to Charity" (accessed November 21, 2017).

9 John Locke, *Second Treatise of Government*, chap. 2, "Of the State of Nature," § 6, and chap. 11, "Of the Extent of the Legislative Power," § 135; Locke, *Some Thoughts Concerning Education*, § 116 (available at Liberty Fund's Online Library of Liberty).

10 Margaret F. Brinig and F.H. Buckley, "The Price of Virtue," *Public Choice* 98.1–2 (January 1999), 111–29.

11 Charles Murray, *Losing Ground: American Social Policy, 1950–1980* (New York: Basic Books, 2015).

12 John J. DiIulio, "The Coming of the Super-Predators," *Weekly Standard*, November 27, 1995.

13 James Madison, Virginia Ratifying Debates, June 20, 1788, in *Debates of the Several State Conventions*, ed. Jonathan Elliot, 2nd ed. (1836), vol. 3:537.

14 Kevin Williamson, "Chaos in the Family, Chaos in the State: The White Working Class's Dysfunction," *National Review*, March 17, 2016.

15 Anne Case and Angus Deaton, "Rising morbidity and mortality in midlife among white non-Hispanic Americans in the 21st century," *Proceedings of the National Academy of Sciences* 112.49 (December 8, 2015), 15078–83; Case and Deaton, "Mortality and Morbidity in the 21st Century," Brookings Papers on Economic Activity, March 23–24, 2017.

16 Eleanor Krause and Isabel Sawhill, "What We Know and Don't Know about Declining Labor Force Participation Rates: A Review," Center on Children and Families, Brookings Institution, May 2017, 20–21.

17 Justin R. Pierce and Peter K. Schott, "Trade Liberalization and Mortality: Evidence from U.S. Counties," NBER Working Paper no. 22849, National Bureau of Economic Research (November 2016), 24, and 43, table 12.

18 William Julius Wilson, *The Truly Disadvantaged: The Inner City, the Underclass, and Public Policy*, 2nd ed. (Chicago: University of Chicago Press, 2012).

19 On the difference between classical and Christian virtues, see Alasdair MacIntyre, *After Virtue: A Study on Moral Theory* (Notre Dame, Ind.: University of Notre Dame Press, 1982).

20 Thomas Frank, *What's the Matter with Kansas? How Conservatives Won the Heart of America* (New York: Henry Holt, 2004), 1.

21 Shelley Garland, "Could It Be Time to Deny White Men the Franchise?" *Huffington Post*, April 13, 2014.

22 Theodore R. Johnson, "We Used to Count Black Americans as 3/5 of a Person. For Reparations, Give Them 5/3 of a Vote," *Washington Post*, August 21, 2015.

23 John Rawls, *A Theory of Justice* (Cambridge, Mass.: Harvard University Press, 1971).

24 *Evangelii Gaudium* (Joy of the Gospel), Apostolic Exhortation of Pope Francis (November 24, 2013), § 198.

25 That's what the utilitarian's standard of maximizing average welfare would do; and the economist John Harsanyi had proposed exactly this before *A Theory of Justice* appeared. The difference between them was that Rawls assumed extreme risk aversion. But that's not how we would choose in real life, said Harsanyi, and that's not the criterion of justice either. For a high payoff in real life, we might be willing to take a risk, and in picking a just society, we'd look at more than maximizing the minimal payout. John C. Harsanyi, "Can the Maximin Principle Serve as a Basis for Morality? A Critique of John Rawls's Theory," *American Political Science Review* 69.2 (June 1975), 594–606.

26 Rawls, *A Theory of Justice*, 15.

27 G. A. Cohen, *If You're an Egalitarian, How Come You're So Rich?* (Cambridge, Mass.: Harvard University Press, 2000).

CHAPTER 16. PASCALIAN MEDITATIONS

1 Blaise Pascal, *Œuvres complètes*, vol. 2 (Paris: Gallimard, 2000), 742–44 (§§ 466–67).

2 Other Pascalians were the Racine of *Phèdre*, the Chateaubriand of the *Génie du christianisme*, Sainte-Beuve, Charles Péguy, Maurice Barrès, Henri Bergson, Georges Bernanos and François Mauriac, a literary tradition with little parallel in the United States, apart from a few novelists such as Cormac McCarthy.

3 On how our hunches efficiently substitute for costly calculation, see Gerd Gigerenzer, *Gut Feelings: The Intelligence of the Unconscious* (New York: Penguin, 2008).

4 Bryan Caplan, "Are Low-Skilled Americans the Master Race?" Library of Economics and Liberty, March 28, 2006.

5 "The problem of organizing a state, however hard it may seem, can be solved even for a race of devils, if only they are intelligent." Immanuel Kant, "Of the Guarantee for Perpetual Peace," First Supplement to *Perpetual Peace: A Philosophical Sketch* (1795), trans. Lewis White Beck, in *Kant on History* (New York: Macmillan, 1963), 112. See further David Gauthier, *Morals by Agreement* (New York: Oxford University Press, 1986); Russell Hardin, *Morality within the Limits of Reason* (Chicago: University of Chicago Press, 1988).

6 Blaise Pascal, *Pensées*, in *Œuvres complètes de Pascal*, ed. Jacques Chevalier (Paris: Gallimard, 1954), 477.

7 Iris Murdoch, *The Sovereignty of Good* (London: Routledge & Kegan Paul, 1970), 70.

8 Numa Denis Fustel de Coulanges, *The Ancient City: A Study of the Religion, Laws, and Institutions of Greece and Rome* (Boston: Lee & Shephard, 1877).

9 Larry Siedentop, *Inventing the Individual: The Origins of Western Liberalism* (Cambridge, Mass.: Harvard University Press, 2014).

10 Alexis de Tocqueville, *Democracy in America*, trans. Harvey Mansfield and Delba Winthrop (Chicago: University of Chicago Press, 2002), 532 (II.ii.20).

11 Friedrich Nietzsche, *On the Genealogy of Morality*, ed. Keith Ansell-Pearson, trans. Carol Diethe (New York: Cambridge University Press, 1997), 20–22 (I.10).

12 A. J. Balfour, *The Foundations of Belief* (London: Longmans, Green, 1893), 83.

13 Immanuel Kant, "Morality thus inevitably leads to religion, and through religion it expresses itself to the idea of a mighty moral lawgiver outside the human being." *Religion within the Boundaries of Mere Reason*, ed. Allen Wood and George di Giovanni (New York: Cambridge University Press, 1998), 35–36 (§§ 6.6–6.7).

14 Jürgen Habermas, *Political Theologies, Public Religions in a Post-Secular World*, ed. Hent De Vries and Lawrence E. Sullivan (New York: Fordham University Press, 2006). See also Terry Eagleton, *Reason, Faith, and Revolution: Reflections on the God Debate* (New Haven: Yale University Press, 2009).

INDEX

Mt. Lebanon Public Library